FORUM FOR SOCIAL STUDIES (FSS)

FSS Studies on Poverty No. 2

Faces of Poverty:

Life in Gäta, Wälo

By
Harald Aspen

Addis Ababa
Forum for Social Studies
June 2003

ISBN: 1-904855-70-9
ISBN-13: 978-1-904855-70-5

Layout by: Mihret Demissew

Table of Contents

Abstract:

Faces of Poverty tells the story of four families in Gäta, South Wälo and depicts their daily lives over a short period of time. The author spent a month in Gäta in 1998, when the area was struck by a long drought and recurrent crop losses. The stories are to a large extent in the words of the people who lived there, providing a rare glimpse of some of the humans behind the grim statistics of poverty and famine in Ethiopia. It is a story about poverty, vulnerability, bad health and lack of education, but most of all it is a story about people and their joys and sorrows, worries and hopes.

Faces of Poverty is written without expert jargon and without attempting to tell a representative story. Illustrated with photographs it makes an easy access to a few lives which certainly are similar with hundreds of thousands of others in rural Ethiopia. In Gäta, the effects of the killer famine of 1984 are still felt. A treacherous climate makes it difficult to rebuild stocks of grain and animals in a subsistence economy. Even relatively good years have "hungry months" when there is nearly nothing to eat. The four families, all of whom are related, may seem to be in an equally bad situation, but at a closer look they appear to be differently endowed with land, draught animals and labour. Past events, unequal ability to work and cyclic household developments, in addition to sheer luck or bad faith, have produced differences between the families and their members which are subtly expressed and dealt with in their daily interactions.

Gäta is a Muslim community with a long history, and it hosts one of the famous Muslim shrines in Wälo. The religion permeates the daily life and the festive occasions, such as the *mäwäkäl* of the oldest member of the little community, an elaborate ritual in honour of the ancestors and Allah. But also everyday activities are filled with blessings, such as the coffee ceremony, and the *du'a* sessions, in which the mildly narcotic *ch'at* is consumed in Allah's honour.

Petty trade is a well established income-generating activity, and we follow the members of the Gäta families, mainly women, to the different weekly markets in the vicinity of Gäta – Kombolcha, Harbu, Ancharo and Adamé. A link to Komolcha, the district capital, is represented by the market and by a daughter who has settled there with her family to live on trade. Through her we also get a glimpse of the urban poverty, and the bonds of reciprocity between the urban and rural relatives.

Acknowledgements

This book is based on fieldworks in Gäta since 1998. I am grateful for the hospitality the people of Gäta offered me. My colleagues Abdulhamid B. Kello and Svein Ege have been there together with me on some occasions and have in various ways given valuable contributions to the work. Svein Ege also produced the maps for this publication. At various stages I was assisted by the late Tolosa Ibsa, Abera Gebrekidan, Meseret Kenfä, Berhanu Bétä, Lesanäwärq Bétä, and Daniel Bägashäw.

In October 2001 I had the opportunity to stay at the Chr. Michelsen Institute in Bergen and to make use of their library and office space. I am grateful to Siegfried Pausewang and his wife Åse, and to the director of the Institute, Gunnar Sørbø, for their hospitality.

The chapter "Husén Ebrahim: a stunted child" is a revised version of a paper I presented at the 14th International Conference of Ethiopian Studies in Addis Ababa 6-12 November 2000 ("A note on life conditions in South Wälo: poverty and infant mortality").

The research work was done as a part of the Peasant Production and Development in Ethiopia (PPDE) project funded by the Norwegian Council for Higher Education's Programme for Development Research and Education (NUFU) and later the project "Rethinking Famine" funded by The Research Council of Norway.

A Note on Personal Names

In Ethiopia, people are referred to by their personal (first) name. There are no family names that survive generational shifts, instead the second name is identical to the person's father's name. Ebrahim, son of Hasän, is therefore named Ebrahim Hasän. In official documents, such as ID cards, it is normal to add the name of the father's father as well. Hasän's father's name was Mariyé Weraqi; thus Ibrahim Hasän Mariyé. Girls also get their father's name, thus Zänäba Hasän Mariyé. In Gäta, some names are very popular, and even among the neighbours in the four houses, they must use the names of the fathers to specify who is addressed. The many women and girls by the name of Fat'ima may alternatively be called Fat'é or Fat'u.

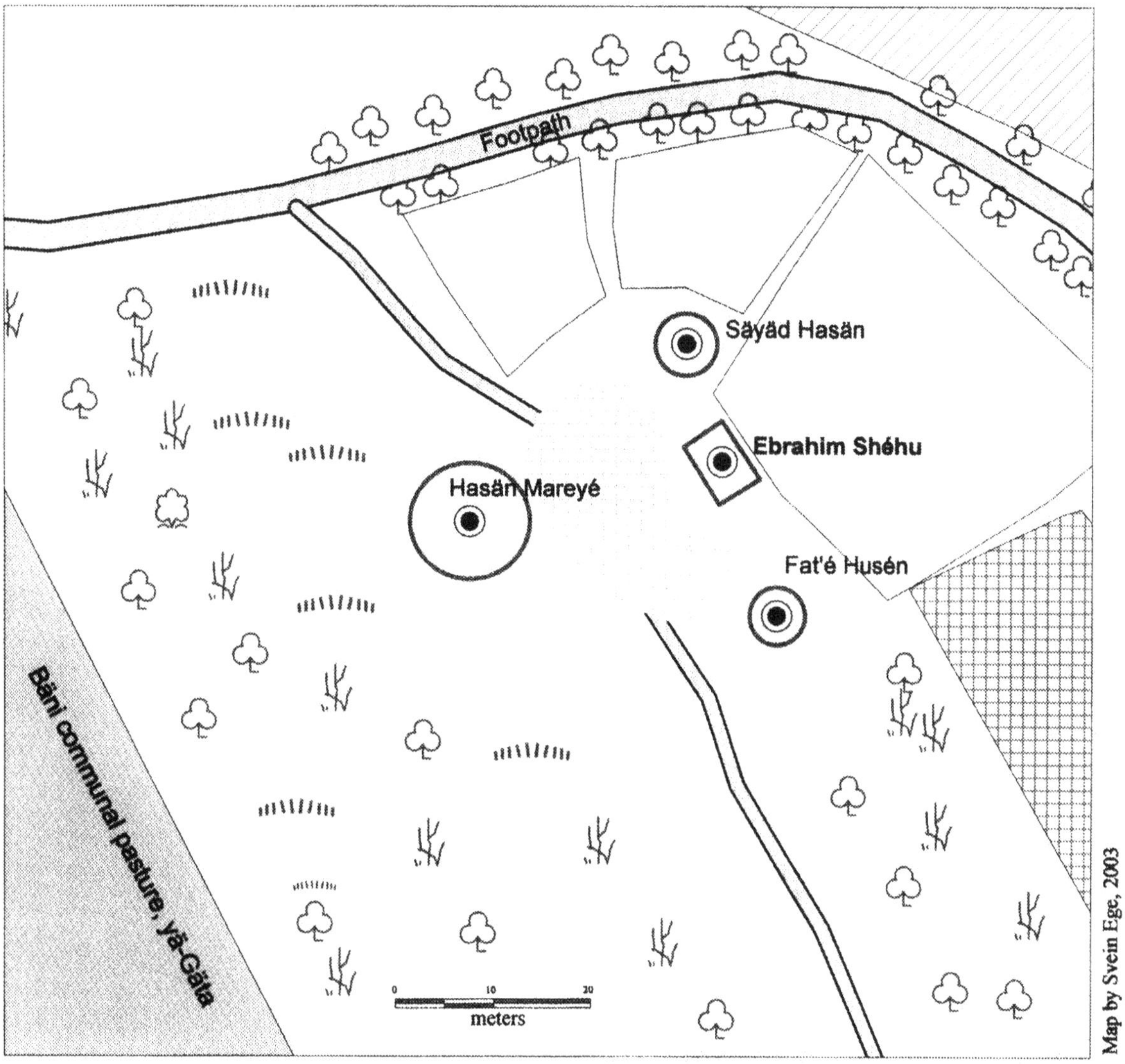
Footpath
Säyäd Hasän
Ebrahim Shéhu
Hasän Mareyé
Fat'é Husén
Bäni communal pasture, yä-Gäta
0
10
20
meters
Map by Svein Ege, 2003

1:750

Ebrahim Shéhu Säyed and Amu Ebrahim
- Zämu (daughter)
- Fat'ima (daughter)
- Jämal (grandson)

In Kombolcha:
Abdu Muhé and Zänäba Hasän
- Mädina and Sa'ada (daughters)
- Zähara Säyäd (Zänäba's niece)

Hasän Mariyé and Kadija Maruf
- Ebrahim (son)
- Zinät (son's wife)
- Husén (grandson)

Säyäd Hasän and Fat'ima Ahmäd
- Indris (son)
- Aminat (daughter)

Fa'té Husén
- Mähamäd (son)
- Aysha (daughter)

Map 1: Ebrahim Shéhu and his neighbours

NORTH WÄLO

Wäldiya

Märsa

Wägäl T'ena

AMBASÄL

WÄRÄ BABO

AFAR

TÄNTA

Tänta

Hayq

KUTA BÄR

TÄHULÄDÄRÄ

QALU

OROMIYA

SOUTH WÄLO

Däsé

Komboïha

Ancharo

QALU

LÄGAMBO

Harbu

Map 2

WÄRÄ ILU

Qämisé

OROMIYA

Wärä Ilu

NORTH SHÄWA

Af'ayé

1:1,000,000

Map by Svein Ege, 2003

Tegray

Afer

Qalu

Amhara

South
Wälo

Beni
Shangul

Oromiya

Gambela

Oromiya

Somali

SNNPRS

Map 2: Location of Qalu wäräda

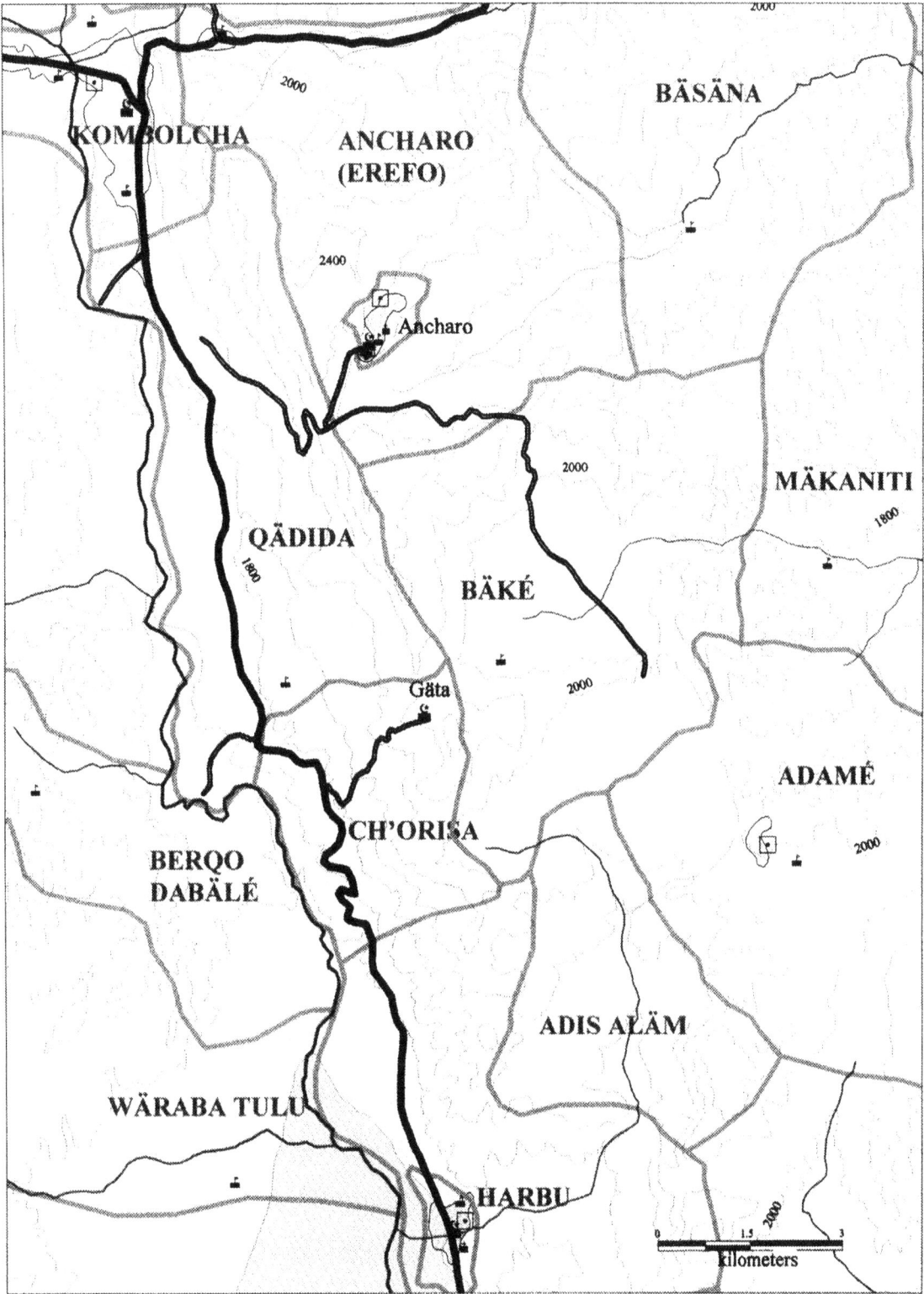

Map 3: Ch'orisa and surroundings

1

Faces of Poverty
Life in Gäta, Wälo

Harald Aspen

The traveller to Gäta follows in the footsteps of thousands of pilgrims who for generations have climbed the same steep paths uphill from the valley below, where the main road from Addis Ababa to the north lies today. It is a tired asphalt road, patched with poor repairs and deep holes, but with regular bus services between the major towns and with minibuses serving as public transport between the small towns of Harbu (south) and Kombolcha (north). A new signboard points to the shrine and mosque in Gäta, announcing that it lies at a 3.5 km distance from the main road. The road to Gäta is rough and stony, steep and with sharp curves, and its steepness and soily sections make it accessible by car only in dry weather. For most inhabitants of Gäta this does not matter much, as there are no public transport services from the main road, and car transport is a luxury for the lucky few and for well-to-do pilgrims who drive their own car or can afford the expense of hiring one. In Gäta, it is only the proprietor of the mosque, *Haji* Muheydin Ahmäd, who owns a car, a small Jeep, but it seems to be out of repair most of the time and the *Haji* travels on his mule, assisted by several servants, down to the main road where he catches up with motorised transport.

My journey to Gäta is not a pilgrimage - I am not seeking God, or Allah, as Divinity is known by the people in Gäta and by the pilgrims. Rather, I seek people, trying to understand what life in Gäta may look and feel like. Neither am I climbing up to Gäta on a crusade against poverty, malnourishment or illiteracy. Like the religious pilgrimage, that is beyond my capacity. But in getting closer to understand life in Gäta, all these aspects confront us: Allah and his servants, poverty and starvation, illiteracy and intellectual isolation.

While I visit the area, I have the opportunity to drive up to Gäta with our four-wheel drive Toyota Landcruiser, borrowed from the Addis Ababa University, safely in the hands of our driver Tecle. He, like the inhabitants of Gäta, finds it difficult to understand why I prefer to walk up on foot along the narrow and steep footpath, which only now and then crosses the broader road. My companion and assistant Tolosa walks with me, without complaints: had he been another kind of person he would surely have cursed me, openly or silently, for this crazy idea of mine to walk when Tecle and the car are at our service. Some days we drive up, and arrive with the noise of the strained engine and shrieking chassis in our ears, not sweating, but unpeaceful at mind. Other days we walk up from the asphalt road, taking a shorter but steeper route than the gravel road. When we start late, at around 7:30 in the morning, the sun is already high and makes us arrive soaked in sweat 50-60 minutes later, at an altitude of about 600 m above the asphalt road.

The path is on hard, dried soil and on stony hills. The climb is arduous and the altitude makes us fight for breath. Small plains between the steep sections give us welcome rest, where we breathe normally even with a higher pace of our steps. I cannot avoid speculating how it must feel to carry heavy loads of firewood and grain up and down this path: we travel lightly with small rucksacks with notebooks and a couple of bottles of mineral water. As we reach higher altitudes, the view over distant mountains and the wide town of Kombolcha gradually appears, and we feel how the breeze becomes cooler than it is down in the valley, which at this time of the year is uncomfortably hot.

The journey is even more straining when it rains – then the hardest soil becomes the thickest and stickiest mud, known as *ch'eqa*. The *ch'eqa* builds up under and around the soles of the shoes, doubles their weight as we go along, slows the speed of the journey, and increases the risk of falling. The inhabitants of the mountains usually do not use shoes in such weather in order to spare the shoes and ease the walk.

It is April 1998, and I am in Wälo for a concentrated fieldwork in a small community that I have visited shortly once before, in November 1997. I am loaded with camera and films, and with information from a survey that my Addis. Ababa University colleagues undertook in October 1997, complemented by two assistants who have worked for me between my first visit and up to the present one. The plan is to settle in Gäta with a tent and sleeping bags, but I realise that the conditions in Gäta, particularly the scarcity of water, will represent a problem. A small but unpleasant health problem calls for good hygiene and plenty of water. For the first time, after a decade of field research in the Ethiopian mountains, I fully realise that I carry my body with me when I do fieldwork – fieldworks in rural Ethiopia are always physical, with stomach aches, foraging mosquitoes and fleas, aching limbs and sunburns, but this is something different. So I give in for comfort and rent a room in Kombolcha's most conspicuous hotel, announcing 24 hours of hot water in the showers, but for days in a row, water is supplied in buckets if you are lucky, and in "Highland Queen" whisky bottles if you are not. So the fieldwork is split between long days in Gäta, in the comfortable shade of a temporary straw hut (*das*) made for our purpose, attached to the house of my host Ebrahim, and in the gentle company of one or several of the inhabitants of the four houses, and the evenings in the relative luxury of Kombolcha. It is not long, perhaps 20 to 30 years, I am told, since the town was little more than a junction of the road (diverting the Asmara and Asäb roads) and a few houses in wide sorghum fields, but it has expanded greatly since then, with an airport, industry, hotels, and wide residential areas. We drive down the 12 km from Kombolcha to Ch'orisa every morning, where the gravel road to Gäta starts, and return in the evening. Sometimes we drive all the way up to Gäta, and on some days we even make the journey twice, assisting our marketing friends with transport. Since this text is about poverty, among other things, it is natural to reflect on the striking contrasts between our evening life in Kombolcha, where we could enjoy a bottle of cold beer for 3.25 birr, and that of young Mähamäd of Gäta, who walked for three full hours all the way to the Kombolcha market, with a load of sorghum stems on his neck, and sold it for 2.50. He bought one *sahen* (a plastic plate used for measurement, containing about 1 kg) of *gwaya* for 2 birr, and added 10 cents to buy a cup of salt for 60 cents, before he returned home with the food to his mother and sister. *Gwaya* is a vetch and its black seeds are considered to be "famine food". It is cheap, but it is known that it may cause paralysis. I shall not tire my readers with pointing to such stark contrasts – the world is full of them for anyone who cares to look. As I said, this is not a pilgrimage, nor a crusade. It is simply a story about four families I have had the pleasure of getting to know, and who generously have allowed me to share their stories and lives with a wider public. As Ebrahim and Kadija, Amu and Hasän said, Allah made us meet, and it is a miracle. If it is Allah's will that we shall appear in a book, then let it be, because then it must be for the good.

Depersonalisation Through Generalisation

Numbers basically represent quantities. They are abstract, and they can be dealt with mathematically in the same manner, regardless of whether they relate to real quantities or not. We have clear ideas about how much five or ten or even one hundred is, because we have direct experiences of such quantities. We see our five left-hand fingers every day, and we know that when we include the right-hand fingers as well, we have the number of ten. Ten is a tangible figure. Hundred becomes more dizzy, but still we have some experience-related ideas about it. A heap of one hundred stones is a heap, but we are still able to identify the individual stones in the heap. It is when we operate with numbers in thousands, or hundreds of thousands or millions, that the individual existence of the items that add up to that number escapes us. The figure becomes sheer mass and sheer abstraction.

As an anthropologist, I sometimes operate with numbers because it is an efficient and universal language with which to express such things as quantities, distances, weight and height, and regularities in relations and structures. All are abstractions, and they belong to a higher-level class of thought that we cannot do without. Like language, it is a code of communication we have agreed to make use of in order to get access to other people's conceptions of the world and to offer other people access to our own concepts and ideas. In the social sciences, there are different traditions for the use of numbers as analytical tools, as instruments to increase our knowledge about how people are related to each other, how they influence each other, and how they depend on each other. My own discipline, social anthropology, is less concerned with numbers and more with a deeper and more holistic understanding of human conditions and human communities. The number-oriented disciplines and approaches are called quantitative, while the other disciplines are called qualitative. There is no sharp distinction between the two approaches, and most social scientists make use of both in varying degrees.

Organisations that deal with large numbers of entities, for example people, are likely to express their aims and goals and programmes with figures. Humanitarian organisations, regional development offices, and states cannot deal with the details of each recipient of aid, each peasant farmer, or each citizen; they analyse how the population can be classified and estimate how many people belong to each category. Then they calculate costs and effects of the operations and programmes they plan to implement. In this process, there is a danger that the numbers attain their own reality, as if numbers, and not human beings, were the objects of the programmes. I do not say there are better ways of doing this; I just say that there is a danger of depersonalising and dehumanising the goal. This text is an attempt to "de-numberise" something which we usually meet as figures, and occasionally, when things go really bad, as photographs and headlines in newspapers and magazines worldwide, depicting people desperate from hunger, women with dying infants at dry breasts and staring eyes that seem to see nothing but death. This story attempts to go beyond the abstractions of figures and the sensations of modern journalism by focusing on four households in Wälo. It is a story about poverty, vulnerability, bad health, and lack of education. But most of all, it is about people, human beings like you and me, with joys and sorrows, worries and hopes. It is about Ebrahim and Amu and their relatives and neighbours who live on a mountain famous for its Muslim shrine and for its vulnerability to the forces of nature, crop failure, and starvation. They live in Gäta, a community in Ch'orisa *qäbälé*, Qalu *wäräda*, South Wälo *zone*, Amhara National Regional State, Ethiopia.

I have two major tools at hand in doing this. One is the language and the words I choose to use, the other is a selection of photographs. Both are representations, and both are subjective – I chose the words, and I chose what to photograph, how to photograph, and what photographs to use. But this is as close as I can get with what I have at hand of instruments and competence. Perhaps the four houses are not what would be called "representative" of the PA or the zone or the region, and in the present context, it is not imperative to know that for sure. Here the aim is simply to describe in words and pictures what life looks like in that small community of four households in Gäta.

Interested readers can find statistical data and other quantitative information on Ch'orisa *qäbälé* in the report *Beyond the Brink of Famine: Ch'orisa 2002* (Ege and Aspen, NTNU, 2003).

Ebrahim Shéhu Säyed

The first time I met Ebrahim and his family was in November 1997. I was on a short "scouting mission" to find a place where I could do an intensive fieldwork later, and I had decided to choose one of three communities in which the research programme I was part of already had conducted the first part of a survey. As Tolosa and I approached Ebrahim's house for the first time, guided by a couple of boys whom we found looking after a few animals at the common grazing land adjacent to the mosque, we registered the pattern of footpaths between the different compounds and the intersecting agricultural plots. The land is stony, but with well-grown trees of various species and big cactuses which are used to demarcate borders and fence plots. After a last, steep climb on a path with loose gravel, a small plateau appeared in front of us, green grass in the middle, four houses, all with their entrance doors facing the centre, distributed in an uneven circle.

A man was cutting a tree in the neighbourhood, hens and roosters were picking what they could find on the ground, and we could see that the door to the house we were told belonged to Ebrahim Shéhu was open. When we called discreetly from outside, as custom requires, a shy and cautious middle-aged woman greeted us as she appeared in the door. This was Amu, Ebrahim's wife. We explained our errand; that our business

4

was the same as that of previous visitors; to ask questions about life conditions here in Gäta. She was not quite comfortable, but she invited us in. Since this obviously was more out of customary courtesy than anything else, we declined the offer but asked for her permission to sit outside for some time and perhaps have a chat with her. Amu was at first reluctant to talk with us; her husband was away attending a funeral; she was sick, and it would be better if we came back some other time. But as our conversation went along, she warmed up and we had a long talk, which gave me the impression of a strong, intelligent and independent woman. When Ebrahim came home from the funeral, we were still with Amu, outside the house, in peaceful conversation, and we had also been introduced to the old married couple in the neighbouring house, Hasän and Kadija, who out of curiosity had joined our little group.

Amu was seriously ill at this time, and she had been unable to move for more than three months: she had a small thorn in her foot and it would not cure. It was swollen and painful, pus drained from the wound, one day from the sole, the other day from above. She was using local medicine, green leaves, and the foot was covered with a piece of cloth and a plastic bag. She said she didn't believe it would help to seek modern medical care, but she had no answer when I pointed to the fact that the traditional medicine did not seem to help either. When we left Amu, I gave her a small amount of money enough to buy ten bottles of beer in Addis Ababa or a box of cigarettes in Norway and she now believes that this money saved her life. She told me how she went to a doctor and was given injections and the wound healed (later she told me another story, though, about how she spent the money on traditional treatment to be cured). She is still handicapped, she does not walk long distances, because she easily becomes short-winded and breathless, and her heart is weak. She said that the real reason for not seeking medical care for the infection was lack of money, but she also feared that the medical doctor might decide to amputate the whole leg. Modern medicine belongs to a different world to which the people in Gäta have scarce access.

Whenever we have met later, during the following years, Amu tends to come back to this episode. With much amusement and relief she will comment on how afraid she was when we suddenly were calling her from outside the house. "I thought you came to take us away from our land", she says, fearing that a new resettlement programme was being launched for the Wälo peasants in the name of development and aid.

This was a time when the harvest from the period of the summer rains (*kerämt*) should have been in house, but the rains had come at wrong times and in wrong quantities, and so the crops had failed. Ebrahim showed us the sad results of this, a *dagusa* stem with no grain, only empty shells. As we left, Ebrahim went with us, showing us the *t'éf* fields that were destroyed by too much rain; when the grain was almost ripe, rains came and made it impossible to harvest, and the ripe grain fell to the earth and was now sprouting in thick mats of green below their tired mother plants. If it could be used at all, it was as cattle fodder. As a prestigious staple food for the urban well-to-dos it could have been sold at the market for good money. Now it gave neither food nor money. Granaries empty, hardship to continue.

5

Ebrahim and Amu have a small house with tin-sheet roof, which is regarded as better than the traditional grass-thatched huts, and sometimes it is used as an indicator of relative wealth by government and development people. Another common indicator is oxen ownership. Ebrahim has no oxen, and would have been classified as "poor" by that indicator but as "rich" by the standard of the roof of his house, if that was the only indicator. In any case, the tin roof is a remembrance of better days, when life was pleasant. The drought and following famine that struck Wälo so hard in 1984/85 (1977 Ethiopian calendar) forced people to sell livestock, which if they had not already starved to death they could only fetch very low prices, and anything else that could be converted into cash that could buy food. In Ebrahim's case, household items, house building materials, and instruments necessary for the agricultural production – all went into the market at increasingly unfavourable prices, compared to prices on food. Ebrahim explained that he would not sell the plough, even if all his animals, including his ox, died. He gave the plough to a relative, perhaps to have an ally when his fields were to be ploughed. It seems that he had not been very actively engaged in agricultural work even before this. Rather, one of his relatives told me, he would spend his time weaving baskets which he sold at the market in Kombolcha. It is not clear to me how, and by whom, his land was cultivated at this time. Perhaps Ebrahim was never a very capable farmer. As we shall see later, he grew up in the mosque as the personal assistant to the *Haji*. Unlike most peasant boys, who live with their family and are gradually introduced to farming by participating in the daily work on the farmland, Ebrahim never had the opportunity of being trained in the skills of agriculture.

Dates and years are not easily remembered when no personal documents exist and there is little else to connect them with. The age of individuals is not accurately registered or remembered; age is usually calculated from some memorable great events, such as "he was born at the end of the time of the Italians", referring to the Italian occupation of Ethiopia (1935-1941), or "she died the same year as *yehadig* (the EPRDF government) came" (1991). The most important event in recent history and peoples' memory is simply referred to as *säba säbat* ("seventy-seven"). This is the year in the Ethiopian calendar when Wälo and the rest of Ethiopia became known all over the world for the drought and thousands of famine victims. "Seventy-seven" in the Ethiopian calendar corresponds to 1984-85 in the Gregorian, which is used in most of the world. The year has 13 months. The first 12 months have 30 days, while the last month, *P'ag^wmé*, has 6 days in leap years and 5 in others. The Ethiopian year starts 7 years and 8 months after the Gregorian, on *Mäskäräm* 1 (11 September). When we refer to years in the Ethiopian calendar, we write "E.C." behind the year. Years in the Gregorian calendar are marked with a "G.C.".

"Seventy-seven" was a watershed in Ebrahim's and his family's lives. "Our house was big, our economy was healthy," Ebrahim recalls. "We had an ox, a cow and a donkey." At that time the family had five members. Ebrahim's mother was living with them, and only the two oldest surviving daughters, Aysha and Zämu, were born at that time.

All his animals died, and to survive he sold a good part of his house, tin-sheets, and wood. The family economy never recovered after that. Now the house has two small rooms in the inner circle and an outer semi-circle that serves as a kitchen for *enjära* baking and a place for the goats. The house is the home of Ebrahim and Amu, their two daughters Zämu and Fat'ima, and their grandson Jämal. Their oldest daughter, Aysha, has recently remarried, but her son from her first marriage, Jämal, lives with his grandparents and has no other wish in life than to stay with them. He is a lively and trusting child, always with a witty and intelligent reply when he is challenged, and no bribe is big enough to divorce him from his grandparents. Ebrahim and Amu teasingly tell him that he should go with me to my country, where he can enjoy good meat, and he replies that if he wants meat, he can go to the *Haji*'s place, the mosque, and the grandparents laughingly tell us that he has been there once at a wedding where meat was served. He can get *yäfäränj dabo*, "white peoples' bread" (loafs of white bread), they say, and he replies that he has got that already, a bread we brought with us from town one day and gave to him and his sisters. Not even a car is anything worth leaving them for, cars can be bought from the market, Jämal self-confidently explains us. And so the play goes between this little entertainer and his enthusiastic audience. The ultimate proof of Jämal's attachment to his grandparents is told many times: he was sent to stay with his mother who lives an hour's walk away, and after three weeks, when his mother was busy somewhere else, he left the house and went the long journey home, only followed by Säyäd, the young son of his mother's new husband, like Jämal about six or seven years old.

I can see, when Jämal's mother Aysha comes visiting, that for her, the coin of love for his grandparents has another side: an indifferent attitude to his mother, almost bordering to enmity. When she calls him to come and kiss her, he refuses to come near her, and he denies that she is his mother. It seems difficult for Aysha to accept this, but in her present condition, she may not have any choice but to accept her son's open refusal. She is married to a man much older than herself, and she lives with him and his three youngest children. I think Jämal is intelligent enough to feel all these tensions and partly wants to punish his mother, who has left him in favour of the others ("Aysha is not my mother, she is Säyäd's mother," he says, referring to Aysha's stepson). Perhaps he also feels trapped between a feeling of loyalty to his grandparents and to his mother, for how can his insistence on staying here be combined with showing love for his mother? Later on, Aysha volunteers to go to the nearby field to chase away monkeys, and Jämal joins her with his sling. On their way back, Jämal's hand finds hers and they walk slowly hand in hand towards the social life at home. Aysha is happy when she returns and tells us that Jämal told her not to walk fast, wanting to make the moment of closeness to his mother last long.

Aysha with Jämal

Jämal's only material possession is the clothes he wears, his wealth is the love he has for his grandparents and which they so lavishly return, and the relation he has to his mother, even if it presently is difficult to show it openly, it seems.

The family seems to live in harmony with each other, even if year-long worries of health and crops and food have made deep imprints in the faces of the older members. The little house is always clean and tidy. There is no furniture – like in most Muslim houses in Wälo, inhabitants and visitors sit on hides on the floor or on the low extensions along the mud walls that make benches. Visitors are received in the front room, while the little inner room is reserved for household members who rest, or do small housework, such as roasting and pounding coffee, cooking, or spinning. In May 1998, we registered every item in the house, apart from personal clothes. We got a list of 33 items, most of which were locally made household materials – baskets, pottery, and wooden implements.

Amu's kitchen

Gäta lies in a mountainous area, facing wild and seemingly inaccessible mountains to the west, gradually sloping down towards the hot and wide lowlands to the east. The landscape of Gäta is intersected with wide, flat alleys with common grazing lands and individual agricultural plots. From the highest point in Gäta, one can see tracts of the country so far away that the Gäta inhabitants do not have names for them.

Gäta had long been a residence for important Muslim families, but the place reached its peak as a centre of teaching and saint veneration with the founder of the present shrine, Sheh Säyed Bushera (d. 1863) in the first half of the nineteenth century. *al-Hajj* Bushera was a Sufi mystic and scholar, who fought against all forms of innovation, strictly adhering to the Sharia law (see Hussein Ahmed's *Islam in Nineteenth-Century Wallo, Ethiopia*, Brill 2001). Lavish gifts from believers have provided the current leader of the shrine, *Haji* Muheydin Ahmäd Haji Bushera, the fourth descendant of the founder, with electricity, piped water, a television set with a video machine, and now a telephone line is about to be installed. I also hear that he is planning to renovate his private quarters, and that a marble floor has been ordered. The piped water no longer serves the rest of the community, which couldn't afford the small maintenance costs, and women and girls spend hours every day to collect water from an open well with unhealthy-looking water: half an hour's downhill walk with empty clay pots (*ensera*), then carefully scooping water into the container, and returning with the heavy load, attached by ropes to their aching backs, by the steep footpath back home.

Haji Muheydin Ahmäd Haji Bushera in front of the mosque

The hills are green during my stay in April 1998, with bushes and trees that represent another tedious task for women and girls, with large baskets on their backs, collecting firewood for their *wät'* cooking and *enjära* baking. In Ebrahim's house, it is Zämu who fetches water and collects the firewood, while her little sister Fat'ima looks after the goats that Ebrahim keeps for the owner, in return for his equal share in their offspring, an arrangement called *rebi*. He has three or four goats by *rebi* and no livestock by his own apart from his *rebi* share of goat kids. Ebrahim sold one of the goat kids at the rural market of Ancharo in early April. The kid was about half a year old, and he expected to fetch 40 birr for it. But as he observed, the market is "full" of sellers in the same situation as himself. Since there were few buyers, the highest offer he got was 30 birr, but he felt he was forced to sell it in order to get money for food for his family.

Gäta lies high enough to be free from malaria, above 2100 m, while the disease is rampant in the lower tracts of the area, including the administrative centre of the *wäräda*, Harbu town.

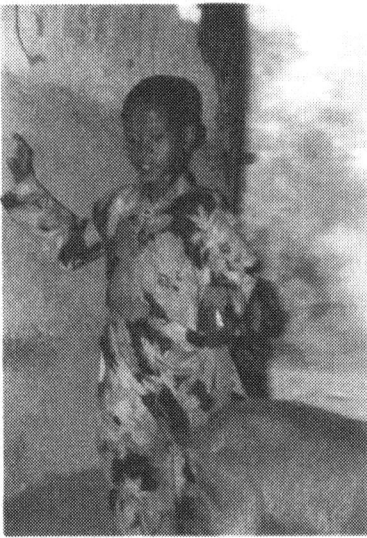

Fat'ima comes in with the goats

Zämu is the hairdo expert. Here she assists Zinät

Hasän and Kadija

The biggest of the four houses in the cluster is less than 10 years old, but it looks much older. Like the two houses described above, it has a grass roof and is circular in shape. It is owned by Hasän Mariyé, an old man whose age we can only estimate from what he tells about his experiences in his life. Hasän is probably about 80. He is the oldest member of this small community, while his wife Kadija is the second oldest. Both have the authority of age, and they are good-humoured and charismatic. Their household counts five members: Hasän and Kadija, and their son Ebrahim, his young wife Zinät, and their 6-month-old son Husèn.

Hasän was married for the first time during the Italian occupation. His wife died two and a half years after the marriage. Their only child, a girl, died when she was one and a half years old. A month after the death of the girl, her mother got sick, and died only five days later, on the 40 days memorial service for the child (*arba qän*). "The *arba* was changed into a funeral," Hasän tells. A year after his first wife's death, Hasän married Kadija. She had also been married once before. Kadija's mother and Ebrahim Shéhu's mother were sisters, and Ebrahim and Kadija call each other sister and brother.

Kadija and Hasän's son Ebrahim Hasän regards the only ox of the household as his, something that his father mildly denies. "Ebrahim is my son, so why shouldn't also the ox be mine," Hasän's argument goes. Hasän applies the same logic to Ebrahim's brother Säyäd and his ox. "They are my sons, so the oxen belong to me." Ebrahim and Säyäd plough their father's plots by coupling their oxen into a pair (*t'emad*), under close supervision by their ageing father.

Säyäd and Indris

Indris

Säyäd has established his own household and occupies the third house together with his wife Fat'ima and their children: Aminat, who is about five years old, and Indris, who is nine. Fat'ima and Säyad have been married for about eleven years. This is Fat'ima's first marriage, while Säyäd has been married once before. Säyäd's oldest daughter from his first marriage, Zähara, used to live with Kadija and Hasän, her grandparents, but four months ago she moved to her father's sister Zänäba, who lives in Kombolcha with her family, trying with her husband to eke out a living from small trade at the market. Zähara's mother left Gäta after the divorce from Säyäd and went to Addis Ababa. The Gäta people know that she went to the capital because she had an uncle there. She married and had a daughter with her new husband. They are also informed that she died about half a year ago. Zähara's grandfather, old Hasän, does not know what she did in Addis Ababa. "perhaps she worked in a *buna bét* (coffee house)," he says, "but I am not sure." Addis Ababa is a full day's travel by bus away, and it takes time before news about people living there reaches Gäta.

11

Fat'é's daughter Aysha mends their house

In the fourth house, a small hut between Ebrahim and Hasän's house, lives Fat'ima Husén, a widow commonly called Fat'é, which we shall also do here, with her two children Mähamäd and Aysha. Widowed ten years ago, she barely subsists on a small plot of land, and with one ox she is able to enter into *mäqänajo* agreements with other one-ox owners, by which two single oxen are coupled into a team for ploughing – a *t'emad* – which means both a team of oxen and the area a team of oxen is able to plough in one day. Her 15-year-old son Mähamäd, a thin, tall boy with a grown-up voice, finds it hard to be the only man of the household, and he is rarely seen in the neighbourhood, busy as he is with firewood cutting, cattle herding, and other male duties. His sister is thin and shy like her mother. Fat'é is thinking of selling her ox, as she has no money and barely any food. Since people commonly seem to value the ox above all other livestock, due to its crucial role for the farming, I wonder why she does not sell her cow instead. She explains that normally this would have been the most sensible option, but her cow is about to calve and that makes a difference. Fat'é and her neighbours are very concerned that livestock prices are falling due to too many sellers and too few buyers. What seems even worse is that an ox-less household has no other option than beg to friends and neighbours to plough for them, or if that does not work, to contract someone with a full ploughing capacity and be left with only half of the yield and none of the stalks of the grain that are used as cattle fodder. This is what Ebrahim does on the major share of his land; a young and strong neighbour ploughs the land in *ekul* agreement. Ebrahim shows us the field while his partner ploughs it, and the *ch'ed*, the straw of *t'éf* from the last harvest that now belongs to the ox owner. While a good season should have given a yield of 15 *quintals*, 1500 kg, the net was only two *quintals* this year, 100 kg for each of the partners.

Faté Husén

Fat'é's son Mähamäd

For many people, including myself, the expression "I have no money" is hardly ever a literal statement. It usually expresses that the money is temporarily scarce and economising is needed. For Fat'é it expresses a real situation. After a market day, we have coffee together with her and some of the other neighbours. Chatting about sowing fields and that it is presently the right time for sowing *dagusa*, Amu asks Fat'é if she has bought *dagusa* seeds for her field. Fat'é says she has not, and when Fat'ima wonders why, she explains that it is simply because she has no money. The price of *dagusa* has increased recently in the market, from two *wälo* (cups) for one birr to three *wälo* for two birr. Fat'é estimates that she needs seeds worth 10 birr to sow her field — money she does not have. 10 birr makes the difference between sowing in time and risking another crop failure due to untimely sowing. Most seeds are broadcast on the soil before it is ploughed for the last time. *Dagusa* is broadcast after the final ploughing if the soil is wet enough after rain. If the soil is dry, it is broadcast twice: before and after ploughing.

Ebrahim has a small field which he calls his *gulma* – a term I know from North Shäwa to mean a land endowment from the family land to a son, which the son ploughs on his own and keeps the produce to save for his future establishment of his own independent household, a sort of advance inheritance. Hussein Ahmed writes in his book that in Gäta, land was called *gulemma* (*Islam in Nineteenth-Century Wallo, Ethiopia*, Brill 2001, p. 93), while Ebrahim specifically uses the term about the plot of land which is his own in all respects because he does not have to share the product with others – he asks ox-owners to plough for him as a friendly assistance, sometimes the sons of Hasän and Kadija (Säyäd and Ebrahim), sometimes others. He estimates that his *gulma* field needs *dagusa* seeds for about eight birr, but he does not have to buy seeds, as he has kept seeds from the previous harvest. Ebrahim often comments how much better it is to have *gulma* than *ekul* fields. The products of the *gulma* are solely controlled by the household that owns it – whenever they like, household members are free to harvest from the land. Not so with *ekul* arrangements: nobody can touch it without the consent and supervision of

13

the *ekul* partner. I feel sympathy for Ebrahim and other ox-less peasants, who commonly complain bitterly how meagre the outcome is when it has to be shared with the ox owner, and I expect the person who ploughs Ebrahim's land to be a comparatively well-to-do person. It appears that he is not; he is a young man with little or no land of his own, who treats Ebrahim with great respect. While Ebrahim can devote his time to other income generating activities (which he actually does not, perhaps due to failing health), the ox owner and his bulls are toiling day in and day out under the sun, risking perhaps a bigger loss than the landowner if the harvest fails, since he also has to feed his oxen. The ploughman is a hardworking youngster who has recently gotten his first child. He invests all his energy in doing the work he knows best, farming, on other people's land. The ageing landowner and the young man at the beginning of his adult life combine their resources for the benefit of both. It is problematic to claim that one of them exploits the other. They are just at different positions in the society and at different stages in their lives.

Also the small spring rains, *bälg*, failed in 1998, and the seeds that were sowed were a net loss. In mid-April we again begin to see cattle graze in *t'éf* fields, and in the expectation of rain – or rather hope and belief in Allah's grace – people replough the fields in preparation for sowing the *mähär* crops. The rain is long due, but the days are hot under the blazing sun, and when dark clouds appear it is only to disappear again without leaving even a drop of humidity. Prayers are made in the mosque, and women gather under wide trees, with small fires for coffee, to make *du'a* – litigations to Allah and his servant Muhammed to bring them rain and food and prosperity. *Ch'at*, the mildly narcotic green leaves of a cultivated bush, is chewed in night-long *du'a* sessions in the *Haji*'s place and in private homes. The delay of the rain is on everybody's mouth, and when people pass fields where the owners are busy ploughing and sowing, exchanges of greetings are mixed with comments about the rain, and the trust in Allah and his mercy. For four consecutive years, crops have more or less failed because of the unpredictability of nature, and Ebrahim comments that it is no longer possible to discriminate between a lazy peasant and a laborious one; however much one works, the result is the same: nearly nil. In fact, the laborious and optimistic peasant expends both his energy and his seeds to no avail and looses more than the lazy ones (but he does not see that this also applies to himself and the ploughman). Farming has become a lottery; the margins between prosperity and disaster are narrow.

The Neighbourhood

These are the neighbours and relatives of the four houses in Gäta. Hardship has reduced social life among them and almost totally cancelled all mutual assistance between them. During the short period in April-May 1998, when Tolesa and I were there, social life was reactivated and our *das* became a common meeting-place for the men and women, boys and girls from the four houses and the neighbourhood. There was nothing to harvest or to thresh, and little to weed, and until the rain came, sowing was out of the question. So there was plenty of time to entertain each other, except on market days. Most of the time, Ebrahim Shéhu was with us, and old Hasän would keep us company on days when he felt well.

Many times almost the whole little community was gathered for coffee in the *das*, or in Ebrahim's house. Sometimes Kadija would invite us for coffee, and sometimes she or Säyäd's wife would bring coffee and an *enjära* to the *das*. Fät'é was never able to return the hospitality of Ebrahim and his guests, Tolosa and myself, and many times this also made her refrain our invitations. Coffee is always followed by a blessing of the host and of the others present; it is usually the oldest participant who prays the blessing. Whenever Kadija was with us at the coffee ceremony, she was given the privilege to bless. Her gracious flow of blessings and beautiful rhetoric made her the unrivalled master of benediction. She would also be the centre of attention in the group at other times, when we had *d'ua* and chewed *ch'at*, or else when we were engaged in relaxed conversations. Her witty tongue and long stories would always catch our attention. Hasän, her husband, was also often asked to conduct the blessing, which he did matter-of-factly and without the eloquence and drama of his wife. Hasän would over-act his old-man-ness and seem strict and authoritarian – qualities that perhaps have to follow his position as the oldest in the compound – but his stern facade concealed a soft heart and sentimental mind. He always longed for those of his children who did not live with him, and particularly for Zänäba. In general, he longed for company and entertainment, and he loved to keep an argument going.

Kadija chewing ch'at, *Fat'é in the Kadija blesses the coffee ceremony background*

Ebrahim belongs to the same generation as Kadija and Hasän but is about 20 years younger than Hasän. Ebrahim seems reduced by his ill fortune, in a way he belittles himself, or perhaps he is made smaller by the circumstances. He is accurate and matter-of-factly in his explanations and narratives, and he is not so inconsistently talkative as Hasän so charmingly is. Ebrahim's emotions are mainly revealed in relation to his wife and children and particularly to his grandson, Jämal.

Amu is in her forties and has been married to Ebrahim for 25 years. Amu is a strong and intelligent woman with authority, but also a lot of humour. Her two youngest daughters, Zämu and Fat'ima are too shy to establish the contact with us that I think they yearn for. Zämu is 23 and very shy, it is almost as if she would prefer to hide, but she cannot conceal her warm and broad smile. She is the one who prepares coffee and food and serves it with humble gestures. Her little sister Fat'ima is about 7, with big, new teeth in her mouth, always with a shy smile on her lips. She was a bit afraid in the beginning, and she was absolutely against being photographed. After some time she utilised her fear for my camera to attract attention and contact, and at the same time keep distance. She seems to prefer to sustain her photophobia in order to keep the play going.

Jämal, Aminat, Amu, Zämu and Fat'ima

Säyäd Hasän's wife is also a Fat'ima - Fat'ima Ahmäd, a light-hearted, humorous woman who applies all her resources to struggle for the survival of her little family. She has given birth to only two children, and she is not happy about this. Her mother in law, Kadija, comments that Fat'ima "has stopped" having babies, although she is still young (she is not yet thirty). Fat'ima's husband Säyäd, a tall and thin man at about forty, has the authority of the oldest son but is still junior in the compound and in the presence of his father Hasän and his neighbour and relative Ebrahim. Säyäd works hard on the fields, together with his younger brother Ebrahim Hasän (and under the close supervision of their father), and with petty trade at the markets, in companionship with his wife.

Säyäd, Aminat, and Fat'ima in front of their house. Fat'ima is grinding grain on the stone mill.

Ebrahim Hasän, Säyäd's younger brother, is married and the father of little Husén, but he has not yet established himself as an independent family head. A happy-looking young man, hardworking as his brother and enjoying married life for his first time, he has always a smile for people he meets. His young wife, Zänit, is about seventeen years old. Her new life as wife and mother cannot hide a young girl's temper and emotions — she alternates between the giggling girl to the etiquette conscious housewife in no time, and she sometimes gets annoyed and angry over the tedious and hard chores that fill her day, like the arduous milling of grain and pulses on the primitive stone grinder in the house. One day I hear her voice call out in a shrilling, annoyed tone: "This is not work for women! It is too hard and boring!", evoking only a knowing and indulgent smile from her elder sister in law, Fat'ima, as if she thinks "well, one day you too will be tamed and realise that this is your life."

Zinät grinds grain on the stone mill

17

Fat'é Hasän, the widow in the fourth house, enjoys being in the company of others, but at the same time she is shy, apparently afraid of being a burden to her neighbours who have just a little more than herself. She is the most difficult one to invite for a meal, and with the exception of food served in connection to rituals; she flees as soon as food is served. But she enjoys the coffee ceremonies and the small talk and occasional stories at those occasions. She is a lovable woman with large doses of rough and sardonic humour, a hoarse voice, and lively eyes. Fat'é's own estimate is that she is about 50 years old. She has been married twice. She hardly remembers her first husband: "I was too young when my parents gave me to him," she says. "I didn't even know how to run a house and knew nothing about marriage, so he got angry and I ran away from him, back home to my parents." When she married her second husband, by the name of Ahmed Muhé (Muhé is a variant of Muhammed), it was of her own willing. She had no children with her first husband but gave birth to nine children with Ahmed. Only three are alive today, the first six are all dead. The oldest surviving daughter, Zämu, has recently married a man in the neighbouring *qäbälé* and left her mother. In principle, the marriage ceremony (*särg*) which is held at the groom's parents' place should have been followed by a return visit (*mäls*) and a party at the bride's place. The scale of the feast (*deges*) depends on the capability of the families, and particularly the groom's capabilities, and in Zämu's case it seems to have been very modest. Fat'é claims that she has never met her son-in-law, she does not even know his name: When he asked for her daughter he did not come personally but sent elders, as tradition commands, and they only told the name of his father, not the boy. Zämu's new husband should not visit his in-laws until he is invited for the *mäls*. "I have not even had time to think about it," Fat'é says, "if we get a good harvest I will plan for it. I will need some money to buy butter, to slaughter a sheep and so on. There will be no *mäls* before we have harvested the crops and only if they are good." Ahmäd Muhé, Fat'é's husband, was the grandson of Kadija's aunt. Ahmäd's land, on which Fat'é and her children now live, was originally given to Ahmäd by the *Haji*.

Like Ebrahim, Fat'é's late husband had been in the *Haji*'s service, and he was remunerated for the services in the form of land. When the revolution took place in Ethiopia, in 1974 G.C., Fat'é and her husband had been living in the harbour city of Asäb in Eritrea for four years (Eritrea was then an Ethiopian province, since 1993 it has been an independent state). The imperial regime fell under the slogan "*märét larashu!*" (lit. "land to the tiller!"), and a large-scale redistribution of land was implemented in 1975 on the basis of a drastic land reform, by which land was registered in the name of the actual tillers. The law regulated the maximum size of the individual landholdings and had other regulations that were meant not only to eradicate the class of landowners, but also the potential for it to re-emerge later. In many areas of Ethiopia, the land redistribution was made with an implicit concern for a just and equal access to land ownership on the basis of need. Land was thus distributed according to household size; large households got proportionally more land than small households. Four years earlier, Fat'é and Ahmäd had left Gäta to attend the mourning ceremonies for Ahmäd's sister's twins who had died not long after they were born. His sister was married in Asäb. Ahmäd asked for work and was employed as a manual worker; loading and unloading ships in the harbour. The land they left in Gäta was ploughed by somebody in an *ekul* arrangement. "We heard that they said *märét larashu*, and we were told that we had to come back and claim our land, so we left Asäb. Because of the situation we came back in convoy. The situation was unstable and the road was bad." Fat'é's household counted six members at the time of the redistribution and was given land accordingly. She still has the land that was measured for them then. The other important capital she has is her livestock: an ox, which is used for ploughing in *mäqänajo* in pair with another ox, a cow, and a male calf. The cow calved during my stay; a healthy female calf. Fat'é wants very much to send her children to school but cannot see how she can manage it. Her son Mähämäd started school but had to leave it in favour of the agricultural tasks he has to attend to, as the only man in the family. "I have nobody to look after the animals and the agriculture except my children. Without animals and agriculture we cannot live or make money – this is the problem, even if I wish my children could get education" Fat'é says.

Sometimes occasional visitors (some are neighbours or relatives, others are strangers who stop for a rest) spend some hours with us in Ebrahim's house; or, if we have installed ourselves in the shade of the *das*, they join us there. Some travellers have a lot to stories to tell, religious anecdotes as well as gossip about people in other areas. Some travel long distances and depend on the hospitality of people on the route, even if they are total strangers. One day, an old man passes the houses, and Ebrahim calls him to stop for a while. He is from around Däsé, and he has walked the whole distance. It took him a day to reach Däsé, where he rested for a few days, staying with relatives. Then he continued the journey from Däsé, he had stopped in Kombolcha with a friend, and then proceeded to Harbu. The hot springs near Harbu town are visited by many people because of its healing effects. He had stayed there for three days, and now he was returning home; hopefully healed from the sickness that had plagued him for more than two months – it was not before now that he had been strong enough to undertake the journey. The stranger tells us that he has finished his provisions for the travel, and Zämu is called to bring him *enjära* and coffee. He is an old and dignified man, obviously a learned man. He presents himself as *Shéh* Ebrahim Säyäd, and soon he is comfortably engaged in one story after the other. He tells about the wife of his host in Kombolcha who has been afflicted by *zar* spirits – they had been peaceful for a long time, but the night he stayed with them she was again possessed, and about the host's daughter who had remained unmarried too long and now was nothing but a dead body. Realising that he has good listeners in our little group, he recites poems about hospitality (a rhetoric device to praise his present host, Ebrahim). One poem is recited many times to give me the chance to write it down. In brief, it deals with the quality of porridge; porridge is such good food that it has to be eaten hurriedly, before others arrive and one has to share it. After several stories about good behaviour and hospitality, he blesses Ebrahim and his family and bids farewell, heading to the mosque and the *Hajj*, whom he knows very well, he says.

Some strangers are not altogether welcome. On one occasion, a *qalicha* – a student of Islam and Koran schoolteacher – seems to appear out of nowhere. All of a sudden, he stands quietly a few metres from the entrance of the house with his covered head bent down. Groups of *qalichas* are commonly seen all over south Wälo, as they usually travel from place to place in small groups, visiting different centres of Islamic training. This one is alone. Dressed in a white blanket (a *gabi*) which covers his whole body and his head, we can hardly see the features of his face. He carries his few personal belongings, the most typical is the little teakettle. There is an aura of threatening mysticism about him. When Amu becomes aware of him, she quietly finds some food and goes out and gives it to him. He receives it and leaves. Not one word has been exchanged. We see the young man walk a few steps up to Kadija's house, where the same exchange is repeated. Afterwards, Amu and Ebrahim complain that the *qalichas* are becoming a burden and a strain on the customary codes of hospitality to travellers. They may be crude and demanding, and an atmosphere of hidden danger looms around their appearance. "It is not a strict obligation to assist travellers," Amu explains, "but Allah has said that it is good to help travellers when one can. We believe it is not good to refuse to give something to travellers as long as we have anything."

Ebrahim and Amu

Ebrahim can remember the time when the Italians left after their occupation of Ethiopia (1941), and on that basis calculates his age to about 60. "I was perhaps of Jämal's age when they left," he says. "I remember there was shooting, and that we were evacuated from here to Mille where we had to stay for three days until we were returned home." Ebrahim's mother Aminat was first married to a man with whom she got two daughters. Both girls died and she left their father. Ebrahim's father was a learned man in Islam, a *qalicha* by the name *Shéh* Säyäd Musah, hence Ebrahim *Shéhu* Säyäd. It appears that Ebrahim's father hardly had lived with his mother. He left her soon after Ebrahim was born and since then lived in Kombolcha. Ebrahim was not raised by his mother, but for 27 years he lived with the present *Hajj*'s father, *Haji* Ahmäd Muhamäd. Ebrahim was the *Hajj*'s servant (*ashkär*) since he was a small boy – the former servant had died and Ebrahim got his chance. He travelled with the holy man to Kombolcha and Däsé, attending the mule and carrying his belongings. "I wasn't very strong," Ebrahim recalls, "but I always walked in front of the mule when the *Haji* moved." During this time, his mother lived alone in Gäta, except for a period when she was married to a man, from whom she later got divorced. She had no children with that man. Ebrahim tells that his mother lived with him and Amu until she died in 1977 E.C. Ebrahim's father died before her, some time during the Därg period. Today Ebrahim has no personal contact with the mosque or its inhabitants. The present *Haji* is the son of the *Haji* whom Ebrahim served. "When I worked there, as the *Haji*'s personal servant, I grew up with his son, we had our food from the same plate. Now we have no contact. I was engaged by the *Haji* personally, this was not government work, and consequently there is no pension," Ebrahim told. "Besides, a son can never be the same as his father," he diplomatically added.

Ebrahim married his first wife while he still lived with the *Haji*, 34 years ago. Zänäba Hasän was her name; she was from neighbouring Bäké Korati. It was Ebrahim's own choice to marry her, so he sent messengers to her parents to ask for her hand. Her parents agreed that he could marry her, and a ceremony called *qebé qäbi* (probably anointing butter on the forehead of the groom) was arranged, a silver necklace (*dämbäl*) was sent to her, and the new union was celebrated. They were married for nine years, but Zänäba did not conceive. "I was longing for a child," Ebrahim explains, "so I divorced Zänäba and married Amu." Amu and Ebrahim have been married for 25 years now, and Amu has given birth to nine children in this period. With the boy she had with her first husband, she has given birth to ten children. **Only three are alive today**: Aysha, Zämu, and Fat'ima.

Ebrahim and his grandson Jämal

Amu was born in Karabété in Anch'aro as the third of eight children. Her father, Ebrahim Mähamäd, died long ago, before the revolution. Her mother, Fat'u Muhé, died only two years ago (1996). Amu's oldest brother died while he was still breastfed. Amu was the second child of her parents. After her, Indris was born; he is married and he and his wife have eight children. Only four of them are alive today. Ahmäd, who was next to Indris, lived in Jimma as a trader, and was recently killed in a car accident there. Occasionally Amu and the others discuss how his property can be claimed by his surviving family; it seems that he had a car and probably a house and other goods. I never found out whether any serious attempt was made by his inheritors, Amu and her siblings, to claim their inheritance. After Ahmäd, two more boys were born, Abdu and Säyäd. Both of them lived with their mother until she died, and they still live together in their mother's house. "None of them have enough money to look for a wife," Amu explains. The youngest child is a daughter, Kadija. She is married with two children.

Amu married her first husband 28 years ago. She had a son with him, but the boy died in infancy. Aysha was born a year after Amu and Ebrahim got married, so she is 24 years old now. Zämu was born about two years after her sister, so she is about 22, and Fat'ima was born in 1981/82 E.C. Amu had twins, a boy and a girl, and then another boy between Zämu and Fat'ima. Like their siblings, who were born after Fat'ima (a boy, then a girl, then again a girl), the children died shortly after they were born (0-40 days is Amu's estimate). Fati'ma was born in 1981/82 E.C., which Fat'é readily confirms: Fat'ima was born at the time her husband died, and that is ten years ago now. "I have given birth to so many children, but I have only three alive," Amu sighs.

In Ebrahim's house, it is the women who have the most regular burden of work. The day starts early, and normally Zämu is the first to get up, at around 5 a.m., followed by her mother and her little sister and nephew. Ebrahim himself, he says, has the privilege to sleep longest. He will not get up before coffee is ready, at around 6.30 a.m. Whenever there is coffee in the house, which is not always the case, it is prepared in the morning. Zämu is also responsible for fetching water, every day she walks twice down to the well with the big clay jar on her back. The water she carries is used for all purposes: drinking, cooking, and washing. The laundry is brought down to the piped water post. Fat'ima spends much of the day in the neighbourhood, herding the goats. Little Jämal has no specific duties yet, but in time he will participate more in the herding of animals together with older children, until he will be responsible himself at the age of 7-8. About his own work, Ebrahim says that "everything has its own season – ploughing, sowing, weeding, harvesting, threshing. In between I will also cut wood. To split the firewood is men's work. Since there is no young man in the house I have to do this. Jämal will be staying here with us, since I don't have my own son. He will be the one who inherits the land."

Amu pounds coffee in her house

Zämu pours coffee

All Ebrahim's plots are adjacent to each other. Apart from the little plot close to the house and the plot which is sharecropped, he has the relatively large plot (three *t'emad*) which he calls his *gulma*. To cultivate this plot he depends on neighbours and relatives with both man- and ox-power. After the long awaited rain finally comes in early May 1998, Ebrahim wants to call for such a workparty (a *giso*). The field has already been sown with oats but the seedlings died. Now he wants to re-sow it with oats or sorghum. The field lies there idle, but Ebrahim fears the costs involved in the *giso* party. The labour is free; although it is expected to be returned when the participants call for work parties themselves, but the workers have to be fed during the day. According to custom, they should be served bread, baked of wheat flour in the host's house, and the wheat has to be bought from the market. When I volunteer to buy the wheat, he decides to call for a *giso*. The date of the event is set to 12 May, and in the days before the workparty the women, not only in Ebrahim's house but also the neighbours, are busy preparing for the event. Wheat is brought to the mill, and bread and *enjära* is baked in unnormal quantities. Totally four teams of oxen plough his field this day. The ox owners operate the plough, while Ebrahim runs after them; throwing away stones and cracking too big pieces of turf that are left in the plough furrow. He is very happy with the arrangement, it seems.

Ebrahim's giso

Infant Mortality

Old Hasän wonders why I spend so much time asking and talking about the dead ones. This is a matter of principle for him, and a source of long discussions in our little group in the *das* whenever the opportunity arises. Hasän denies the value of history and remembrance of the dead ones, and he cares nothing about being photographed for the benefit of his surviving relatives. "If they want to see me, they can visit me," he says. "When I'm gone, I'm gone." All of us disagree with him, and I argue that he enjoys telling stories about past years and events and people who are long dead, so history is of great value also to him. When he says this is his form of entertainment I say that it has educational value for the younger generations – they can learn from history, I say. Old Hasän is uncompromising in his rejection of history, but at the same time I think I can detect something sore in him when this issue is raised. I never understand what it is or what the cause might be; but I guess it is complex issue. Firstly, there is the frustration over getting old and infirm and unproductive, a fact that Hasän challenges with at least two different strategies: One is to argue that he has worked hard for many years, and that the new generation, his sons whom he has raised, now has a moral duty to feed him; a second strategy is to make himself busy and "productive" by taking the role of landholder; supervising and ordering his sons and grandchildren in their agricultural tasks. Secondly, there is the feeling of impotence and incomprehensibility when confronted with the dramatic political changes in his lifetime: the revolution and the land reform, the long civil war, and the victorious EPRDF government. Hasän seems to have doubts about the new generation's wish to seek advice from knowledgeable elders, logically enough, when local positions of power and responsibility are in the hands of the youngsters, and young people deal with their elders as if they were equals, disregarding established etiquette of deference. I believe Hasän is sore because the dignity and honour that should follow old age seems to have been eroded and forgotten; yet another right that has been snatched from him in the course of history.

Apart from his peculiar argument and principle, Hasän shares with his relatives and neighbours his unwillingness to talk about the dead ones, and especially the prematurely dead. It evokes destructive feelings of sorrow and longing for no good reason. I must admit that I am so preoccupied with infant and child death because where I come from, in my country; it is extremely rare that babies or children die. So why is this so common here, I ask innocently. As if that is so hard to understand! The health and diet of the mother, the lack of qualified health personnel, lack of modern medicine and modern medical expertise, lack of food, lack of knowledge, lack of hygiene. My companions are just as wondering as I am, but with the opposite perspective: is it true that children do not die in Norway? How come? Ah, as if they don't know: enough food, enough health, enough medicine, enough knowledge, enough strength. Another world. But here in Gäta there are several layers of explanation, because despite all these lacks and needs, many children do grow up, although against heavy odds. So how can this be explained? Amu and Fat'é explain to me that if a woman who gives birth to a child has *aynä t'ela* (lit. "the shadow of the eye", a spiritual affliction related to the evil eye), the child is doomed to die before forty days have passed. In such cases, the parents are advised not to bother with circumcising the child, which is normally done when the child is seven days old. It is believed that the *aynä t'ela* rests in the bed that is prepared for the woman in confinement and waits there for its victim. This is a disease (*bäsheta*) that comes to households who have failed to arrange ceremonies such as the annual *mäwäkäl* in the honour of the spirits and forefathers. This spiritual explanation of disease does not contradict explanations that we readily accept as rational; it just adds a dimension to them.

Child mortality is a highly relevant topic in Gäta. In addition to Fat'ima, Säyäd Hasän's wife, who has only given birth to Endris and Aminat, both of whom well and healthy, it is only young Zinät who has not yet experienced the loss of a child. But her little son Husén is stunting and seems very weak, a fact that is not left uncommented by the other women. "A child of his age is normally very active, and would have started to creep by now," they say, in the presence of the mother, "this one is really very weak, he can hardly sit upright on his own." Husén is in his sixth month, and despite his weak appearance with his unstable head on his extremely thin body, he has a strong voice which can be heard most of the day from Kadija and Hasän's house. He cries and cries, unsatisfied perhaps, instinctively calling for attention from his young mother. The simple explanation I am offered is that he is "sick". As time passes and my involvement in little Husén Ebrahim's health increases, his sickness becomes a multidimensional phenomenon that can serve as one illustration of what a "stunted child" can be.

Husén Ebrahim: A Stunted Child

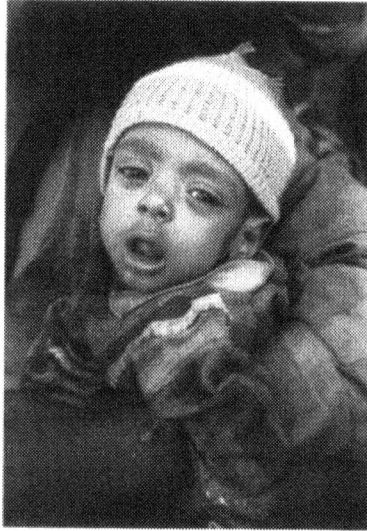

Husén Ebrahim

The desperate crying of little Husén is emotionally disturbing. It is obvious that he has a problem, and it seems to me that he will die if there is no change in his condition and/or in the treatment he is offered. I have tried to figure out what is wrong with him, and I have been told that he is sick from time to time. Zinät, his 17-year-old mother, lives with her husband Ebrahim and her parents–in-law, Kadija and Hasän, in their house. The three other households, and the experienced mothers in each of them, are also very close to Zinät. So, I reason, it cannot be lack of advice and instructions that has caused the problem. True enough, Zinät is young and inexperienced as a mother, but the child's grandmother and aunts are not. But at the same time I find it curious that the other women seem to leave much of the worries and responsibility for the child with Zinät, as if they do not care much about the wellbeing of the baby. The father hides his worries, and when he is asked about the health of his son, as custom requests of visitors, he happily replies *"shäga näw"* –he is very well – also a customary reply. The boy's grandfather, old Hasän, seems to be both pessimistic and fatalistic in his comment that one should leave such things to Allah – if it is Allah's will that the boy should grow up, he will survive; if it is not, one should let him die without spending energy and money on searching for a cure. This comment annoys me, and I argue that he also works hard to feed himself, to keep himself alive – he does not at all put the whole responsibility in the hands of Allah. So why should we do that for little Husén? For one rare occasion, Hasän gives in and admits that I am right, but I can see he is uneasily withholding further arguments. There is something I do not fully understand here, I just see a fragment of it, but it is important and it is connected with the apparent indifference of the experienced women. I believe it embarrasses Hasän when he realises that I do not understand, that I cannot see, what is so obvious to them. Today I think I know what it is. Where there are hardly any resources, priorities must be made. A child which is weak has small chances to survive in the long run in this harsh situation. Even if all resources are spent on a cure and the child survives, it may never get strong; it may die of the next crisis, or it will remain a burden on its family. There are better uses of scarce resources than placing them on weak bets. Investments have to be made on as safe stakes as possible.

But where there is no money, money cannot be spent. When I inquire about treatment and medicine, I am told that he is treated by a traditional *Abäsha hakim* – a local healer, who has given him something to drink and to put in his ears. Zinät says she does not take the risk of travelling with him to Kombolcha to seek modern medical advice, as she fears it will be too warm for the boy, and at this time, end of April, it is very hot down in the valley. There is also a more or less expressed concern that Kadija and Hasän are against modern medicine, but when I ask Hasän, he says that this is an issue he leaves to the parents of the child to decide. We have brought the car with us up to Gäta this day to collect Ebrahim and take him with us on a car drive to the market in Ancharo, the old *wäräda* capital. When Zinät, after the usual greetings with Husén limp in her hands, asks me for medicine, events develop fast. I offer her a ride down to Kombolcha in the car, protected from sunshine and heat, and transport back. If she worries about expenses, I will cover them. Her sister-in-law, Ebrahim's elder sister Zänäba, lives in Kombolcha and she can also assist. Zinät is not certain, and we leave her to think about it. We call her father–in–law, who sits at a nearby field, watching (or rather supervising) his son Ebrahim's ploughing. Hasän confirms that he is not against modern medicine – and we laugh when we remember Amu and her fear when she had the wound in her foot. Fat'ima, who quickly has appreciated the topic of our discussion and has gone up to Zinät to talk with her, comes back and reports that Zinät has agreed to go with us, and that Fat'ima will join us to assist and comfort the young mother. It has been one of my worried concerns for several days now, how to convince Zinät and the others that the boy needs medical attention, without imposing myself too much upon them and their patterns of authority. Now everything went smoothly.

We are uncertain where to go in Kombolcha. There are a couple of private clinics, one of which lacks a laboratory and is regarded secondary to the other, and there is a public health centre which is run by the Mekane Yesus church. I realise that Fat'ima knows all the options – she has only two children of excellent health, and her family is in many regards of a better standing than Zinät's. We decide to go for the Mekane Yesus compound, where the morning scene is depressingly familiar: Sick people and their assistants waiting in groups in the open and at the balcony, attendants in white uniforms

26

sorting and ordering the clients about. We arrive in the large landcruiser and park it in the shade of a tree, and while Tecle waits in the car the rest of our entourage – Zinät with the child, Fat'ima, Ebrahim Shéhu, Tolosa, and myself advance towards the clinic. An attendant approaches us and asks politely what we need, and I ask where the doctor can be found. I am readily shown to his door, which is held open for me; and it is only when I halt at the doorstep to let the others pass before me that I detect a flicker of surprise in the attendant's face, as he realises that it is not me but the locals that came with me that needs the doctor's attention. The doctor is professional and friendly, and he lets nothing reveal any surprise, if there is any, over the unusual group that suddenly fills his little office. When he sees the child he immediately says that "oh – this child is sick, no doubt about it." He listens to my explanation and request, briefly examines the child and directs a few questions to the mother, before he sends us to the adjoining room where mother and child care is carried out, including vaccinations. A male nurse readily receives us there. He weighs Husén, and with an almost abstracted professionality he declares that the boy is seriously underweight, probably due to under- and mal-nourishment. He takes his time and works routinely with mother and child, but in the middle of the proceedings, he directs a question to Tolosa and me: "Are they mountain people?" (*yätärara säw nachäw?*) When we readily confirm that, it is as if invisible threads have been spun which bind the three of us – the nurse, Tolosa and myself, in a web of communality. We nod knowingly to each other: They are mountain people. We are not. They are poor, ignorant, unhealthy. They are what we are not. The disassociated attitude of the nurse was perhaps an aspect of his professional attitude, and his unsentimental appearance perhaps a part of his mental survival kit, so to say. But the difference which characterises the "mountain people" contributes to both ways of creating distance between the patients and the health workers.

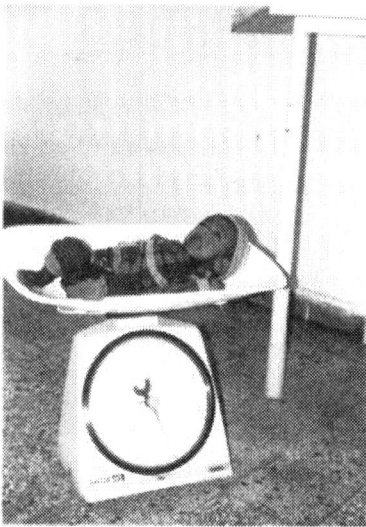

Husén on the scale

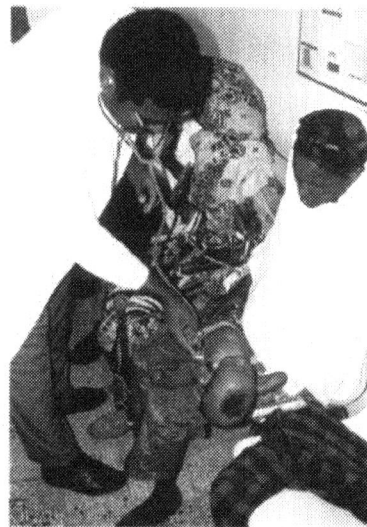

The doctor examines Husén

Husén weighs only about 4 kg, and the nurse shows us on the boy's new health card (the first in his life) that he falls well below even the lowest range of the medium growth graph. The nurse does not even try to hide his disapproval of Zinät when he interviews her about the boy. "Has he been vaccinated?" he asks, and when Zinät fearfully shakes her head, he immediately follows up with a "Why not? Don't you know the vaccination programme? Don't you have that where you live?" And Zinät has to admit that she does not know why, and that there is a vaccinator down at the asphalt road in Ch'aqorti, and so on. Her eyes become wide open by fear when the nurse tells that he is going to give the boy some injections, and he starts filling syringes from small bottles. First he gets three drops in his mouth, then an injection in the thin, wrinkled arm, and the last one in his bottom. The boy cries loudly and Zinät, who holds him and tries to comfort him with her breast, seems to be on the verge of crying herself. The boy soon calms down when the nurse has vaccinated him, now it is Zinät's turn. The nurse does not even ask her, he just tells her that he is to give her an injection and explains that they routinely vaccinate women in their childbearing age against tetanus. Zinät becomes even more disturbed and wants to cry, and she is only calmed down when we argue that if Husén could stand two injections, she must manage one. She agrees, and turns away from the nurse and his syringe, seeking comfort from Fat'ima who sits with her. The injection is over before Zinät has finished fortifying herself against it. "Is it over?" she asks unbelievingly. "Was that all?" And she laughs, relieved, and a little ashamed that she made such a fuss out of nothing.

We return to the doctor with the papers, and he concludes that the child is not sick from anything else but too little, and wrong food. Zinät, already adapted to the situation and relieved that things have gone well so far, explains that she breastfeeds him but fears that she does not have enough milk for him. The doctor explains that she should give him cow milk and porridge, and asks if they have such things. Zinät confirms that. The discussion about the cow and the milk and the lack of food seems inappropriate here in the doctor's office. It will not make any difference in any case. Then the doctor starts talking about prevention and family planning, but Fat'ima soon interrupts him and reveals her very pertinent, but perhaps, in the present situation, rather inappropriate question: "What can I do to have more children? Can you advise me how to conceive?" upon which the doctor tells her to come back some other time with her problem, and we are dismissed. Then, relief and surprise over how fast things went, and all of us know we were treated favourably for one reason: my presence. And we also know that had I not been there, the group would still have had quicker access to treatment due to the symbols of belonging to "them", the rich and educated; the Toyota Landcruiser, the behaviour, language, and clothes of Tecle and Tolosa. The fact that we did not pay a single cent for the service also seems to be a bit of surprise and relief, at least to Zinät. Fat'ima is much more experienced in this, and later she tells us that she has followed the vaccination programmes for her own children since they were born.

It seems that Husén improves after this, not because of the vaccinations, but because Zinät feels that she can seek advice about food and treatment, and I feel that I now have the license to take a much more active interest in Husén's health than before. A couple of days after the visit to the health centre in Kombolcha, Zämu and Amu serve us a rare *alecha* (unpeppered) meal of meat and vegetables with the *enjära*, and I take the opportunity to show Zinät one kind of food for her baby, by crushing some of the vegetables with the soup in a cup and feeding him with a teaspoon. The boy eats heartily and the mother and her inlaws express their admiration for this invention. Perhaps they do this out of sheer politeness, or they are genuinely surprised and pleased, none of which really matter, because I know with them that such food does not exist in either of the households when I leave and normal days return.

The others in Zinät's family seem to be positive to the modern medical treatment the boy has been given in the Kombolcha health centre, but still a sense of dissatisfaction lingers on. The boy's grandmother, Kadija, and his aunt in Kombolcha, Zänäba, indicate now and then that the traditional medical treatment the boy had already started should not be discontinued. Butter and green leaves continue to be applied on top of his head, and new calls for medicine come when he becomes plagued with pus in his eyes to the extent that he cannot open them in the morning. Zänäba tells her mother that he should have been brought to a knowledgeable woman in Kombolcha who has specialised in healing children.

Husén and his aunt Zähara

Almost four years later, in February 2002, Zinät again has a baby at her breast, a strong little boy by the name Abdu Ebrahim. Abdu is Zinät's third child. A baby girl was born some time after my stay in 1998, but she died shortly after, like so many others. Zinät started using contraceptive pills after Abdu was born. "Two children is not enough," she says, "but it is good to make a two year gap between the children. I learnt a lot from the experience with Husén." She wants to have four or five children, she tells us.

Every time we meet I am praised because I "saved Husén's life". At this occasion, Zinät recalls how it was when her firstborn child almost died: "I was desperate and feared that Husén should die. I did not know what to do, I carried him with me and had to listen to people whom I met on the road. They said to me that I should just leave him in the house and let him lie there and let him wait until his soul leaves him – there is nothing that can be done for him. I always remember you, you will always be in my heart for what you did for my child," Zinät says. "It is common that children die here, either immediately after they are born or at the age of 2-3. Previously we had no belief in modern doctors, so when children fell ill, they often died. It is a new thing that we believe that the doctor can give medicine and save life."

At the age of four, Husén is a lively and strong boy. Fearless he moves with the older children when they water the animals, carrying his own stick. It seems that it is only one thing that can frighten him: the *färänj*. Everybody calls him when I am around: "Husén, come and greet your father! He is the one who gave you your life!" And Husén screams and runs away, apparently terrified by my presence. Perhaps he believes that I am here to take his life away again?

Zinät's sister-in-law, Fat'ima, who asked the doctor for advice on how to conceive, is also happily carrying a baby girl, Lulaba Säyäd. Her third child was born at last, after many years of longing for more children. "People thought I used the pill," she says, "but I never did. I always wanted more children and I was afraid I would not have another baby, but with the help of Allah I finally got this one." I ask her if three children are enough: "If Allah permits me I would like to have more children, especially a boy," she replies.

Virginity

"Yes, a woman's life consists of hard work and pregnancies," say Amu and Fat'é – "what else is there? If she divorces and marries another man, life remains the same – it will be the same difficulties. As soon as we get children, we are trapped – we have lost other opportunities and chances." And our discussion takes us to another value in women, that of their virginity. When Amu, Fat'é, and Hasän talk about the increased strictness and value attached to virginity, they say things I have already heard from Ebrahim and other men one day when we went together to the Adamé market. Previously, they tell me, some men would cover the fact that their new bride was not a virgin. Instead of sending her back to her parents, and bring shame upon herself, her parents and her groom, the groom would cut himself in the leg to draw blood and stain the bedsheet with it as a proof of the girl's virginity. Not so anymore, now the girl will be chased home the same night, or at the latest the next morning, and the groom and his family will request a compensation. The girl will be sent home almost naked; there is no urge to keep the shame a secret, what people want is the compensation, says Hasän. A commonly mentioned amount these days is 3000 birr, a fortune for the claimant and a disaster for the sued person. Hasän explains that the cheated husband will beat the girl until she reveals who took her virginity, and he is the one who is forced to pay compensation (or rather his father is). If he does not pay, the girl's family will be forced to compensate. Usually, elders are used to make the decision about the compensation. People who are exposed are forced to sell their animals and other belongings to pay the amount to the insulted party. The disgraced girl, despite her loss of respectability and popularity, will usually be married again. It is usually at the first marriage a man should marry a virgin, most of the time an arrangement between the man's family and the family of the girl. It is a young man's *aqli* (luck) to be married to a virgin.

The fact that I heard this from different persons, but with almost identical elements, may indicate that it is not really a common occurrence, as it is claimed, but rather a good history. I never tried to check the story by asking who had experienced it, when it had happened, and such things. If it were as common as it was claimed, one would have expected the histories to differ from each other, and not appear in different contexts in exactly the same form. Certainly, there must be a grain of truth in it, and it is a good story, since it emphasises the desperation in the community when resources are so scarce. At the same time, it surprised me that virginity had become such a potential source of monetary compensation. First, a compensation of 3000 birr seemed to me an outrageous amount in this community. Second, compared with the position of women in North Shäwa, I found the women in South Wälo to be much more independent, relaxed and free – which in my opinion did not fit with very strong control mechanisms such as the threat of huge compensations and the deep shame connected to premarital sex.

If the first marriage is broken, which is a common occurrence, the divorcees have much more personal freedom to find their next spouse. In this society, where there are some strict rules of segregation regarding men's and women's work, the sexes are bound together in a mutual dependence. It is particularly difficult for men to live without a woman in the house, for who shall fetch water, clean the house, and cook the meals? Certainly not the man. On the other hand, women cannot plough the land; that is a male monopoly. But it is easier for women to maintain their life without male hands in the house, because male labour can be rented through various arrangements, normally by sharecropping. Thus, households with only women and girls are not uncommon, while a *yä-wänd bét*, a "male house", is a miserable and short-lived rarity. A man, if he cannot find a wife or a female servant, may live with a daughter, sister, or mother.

Monogamy or Polygamy. Husband and Wife

Islam allows men to have four wives at the same time, and Ebrahim tells that before "seventy-seven", the famine, it was common in Gäta that men had more than one wife.

Hasän married a second wife while he was married with Kadija. It may not be difficult to understand that Kadija disliked this arrangement. Amu comments that the second wife, Muntah Kämal, was not on good terms with Kadija, so she divorced from Hasän after some time. Muntah was about the same age as Kadija, and she got a son, Mähamäd, by Hasän. Mähamäd is now on *zämächa*, "campaign", which means he is a soldier in the army. Kadija becomes excited when we discuss this. "None of his relatives liked that he married her, everybody was angry at him. I had a disagreement with him and I left him and went to my own family, and when I was there, he married the other one. His relatives didn't like this and advised him to "divorce that woman and bring Kadija back!" While I stayed with my relatives, Hasän ignored his work – because he was in love with this woman the crops were destroyed by pests and birds!" The discussion is lively, everybody has an opinion about this period in Kadija and Hasän's marital life, and Hasän seems to enjoy listening to the women's narrative about his youthful and manly vigour, even if they led him astray for a while. He humorously and self-confidently comments: "If I get rich I marry many women, if I get poor I chase them out." At the same time he distances himself from his statement by providing us with a saying in Amharic:

"If the lord becomes rich, he buys land.
If the peasant becomes rich he marries a woman."
(lit. "he buys a wife")

Muntaha

Muntaha Kämal and her daughter Fat'é are neighbours and regular visitors of Amu and Ebrahim, and Kadija and Hasän. Muntaha is related to Ebrahim and Kadija, but it is hard to find out exactly how. Muntaha's memory is failing, and my insistence on accuracy in these matters seems to be unusual and confusing. She refuses to try to remember how old she was when she first married, she was married to another man before she married Ebrahim's relative. Hasän, probably as a qualified guess, suggests she was about 12 years old when she was first married. We spend hours and days on the genealogies of the members of the four houses, and on Muntaha's relation to them. For the sake of simplicity, Muntaha normally passes as the wife of Kadija and Ebrahim's uncle. After struggling with more accurate genealogies, we agree that Muntaha is the widow of Ebrahim and Kadija's common grandmother's brother's son. Kinship is an important dimension of alliances and social structures in all societies, and social anthropologists always try to map out the genealogical connections between people. In trying this, we often encounter the difference between what is genealogically correct and what is workable for people: Ebrahim and Kadija are cousins, but regard themselves as siblings, which also symbolically loads their relationship with more affection and closeness. Muntaha is in principle a rather distant, affinal relative, i.e. a relative by marriage, but in the daily interaction, she is regarded as an uncle's wife, which has the same effect with regard to the symbolic value of the relationship she has with her neighbours. This both welcomes her to the intimate sphere of close kin and explains her presence in this sphere.

Muntaha

Muntaha's daughter, Fat'ima

Muntaha is about 75 years old, her daughter about 50. They live alone in a relatively big house in a fenced compound. Both are very thin. Muntaha has given birth to five children, of whom only two are still alive. In addition to Fat'é, who lives with her mother, she has a son who lives in Harbu town, where he works as a tailor. "He is getting very thin. He doesn't even have enough for himself and his family, he has so many children," Muntaha says. "I have advised his wife to stop getting children, but she refused." So there is no support to be expected from her son. The little land she owns is shared in an *ekul* arrangement with a sharecropper (the harvest is shared equally between the two partners). "My share was two donkey loads (one *ch'enät*, donkey load, is approximately 50 kg) of sorghum (*ch'äräqit*, a very white variety), and in addition to grain, we also need salt, spices, and so on. So you understand our share of the harvest doesn't last for many days." It is a mystery to me how Muntaha and Fat'é survived. What is certain is that they must be living from hand to mouth, from day to day. When I asked Muntaha when what her best period in life had been, she bypassed the question by simply stating that she did not remember, and besides, "I don't work any more, I am totally dependent on my daughter. I am grateful to Allah that I am well and that I have a good life. We asked Allah not to bring us the worst, and Allah will keep us, so that we will not see things worse than they currently are." A detour, in other words: to say that things are really bad, but we should be glad as long as they do not get even worse. Despite her misery, Muntaha is a woman of principles. She is known not to drink coffee outside her own home because she hates low quality coffee. In many homes, the only coffee that is served is made not of coffee beans but of the much cheaper husks of the beans, which are sold at the markets in South Wälo in larger quantities, it seems, than the proper coffee. As long as I stay in Ebrahim's house, however, I make sure that we have sufficient supplies of the best quality coffee that is for sale in Kombolcha (at prices of 17-18 birr per kg, it is simply not accessible for my hosts if they were to provide for it themselves). So Muntaha joins us regularly, sometimes also with her daughter, and breaks her own principle and enjoys our coffee and its affiliated ceremonies. And as has become so normal during these difficult times, making her accept an invitation for food is almost impossible. Like our neighbour Fat'é, it is only a small piece of bread or *enjära*, with no stew (*wät'*) but sometimes with some *bärbäré* (powdered red hot pepper), butter, or oil, served as an almost ritual snack with the coffee (*buna qurs*), which is accepted after long persuasions by Zämu or Amu and the rest of us.

Fat'é and Muntaha are the two most difficult persons to invite, and it is obvious that the reason is their inability to return the hospitality. Fat'ima, Kadija, and their husbands usually accept such simple invitations. Return invitations occur regularly, perhaps twice a week. Coffee and some food may be brought to the *das,* or we are invited to their house. There are only very few visual signs of difference between the households, Fat'é's and Muntaha's are visibly the poorest – the family members are thinner, and they are more difficult to invite. The house of Fat'é is perhaps the smallest (but Säyäd and Fat'ima also have a rather small hut), or it only appears to be simpler than the others – it is hard to pinpoint concrete details, but it looks more worn and unmended. The outer kitchen is built of simpler materials and closed with simple sorghum stalks, and even if I observe one day that her daughter Aysha is mending the outer walls with fresh cow dung, the walls look tired, perhaps a bit skewed. Muntaha has a relatively large house in a fenced compound, but it looks deserted; inside it is almost empty.

In comparison, Säyäd's house, even though it is small, gives a solid impression; it is well mended and organised. Fat'ima, his wife, and the two children are healthy-looking, well built and not very thin.

Fat'é and Muntaha do not represent a different class from the others, and they are relatively well endowed in land (even if they have little *t'emad*), and Fat'é even has livestock (an ox and a cow). But they are at particular stages in their life careers – Muntaha at the very end of her life, Fat'é in the age of "retirement" as her son Mähämäd is about to take over the responsibility as the head of the household, including being registered as the land owner (and land tax payer) in the *qäbälé* tax lists. The other households, except from that of Ebrahim Shéhu, have more and better distributed manpower than the others. Säyäd and Fat'ima are at the height of their life: a strong man who can plough the land and do other heavy agricultural work, a strong woman responsible for the household chores and active in trading, and two children who are old and healthy enough to water the animals and herd them when they are grazing. While the two old women lack all these capacities (Fat'é is relatively active at the markets but stays home now and then due to a failing health), the well-composed families are able to broaden their economic activities.

The fact that Fat'é and Muntaha are women may influence their reluctance to accept invitations, perhaps because they are more concerned about the stock of food available at any given time, compared to the men. They are also not close relatives, and this reduces their moral "claim" to assistance from their neighbours. Kadija often complains that the social life is very much reduced now, compared to the "good old days" when they had plenty of everything. Fat'é has experienced another life, as a salaried worker in the town of Asäb. Muntaha, even if she refrained from making any judgements about which period of her life had been the best, must also have been used to a better life at some stage – her distaste for low quality coffee, and conversely, her liking for good coffee, must have been acquired at some point in her life, when such present-day luxuries were accessible also to her.

Mäwäkäl: A Tribute to Allah

The Gäta people inhabit a world that they share with spirits and ancestors, powers of good and evil. Small and big rituals are therefore an integral part of daily life in Gäta, like elsewhere in Ethiopia. Apart from the rituals common for Muslim believers, which individuals in varying degrees follow, there are also rituals that are connected with the wellbeing of individual persons or families and which are conducted privately. *Mäwäkäl* is a semi-private ceremony of this kind, a ritual to thank Allah for bringing what one has prayed for during the last year. The ritual should be conducted annually, and failure to do so may cause the wrath of the ancestors, resulting in ill health or other misfortunes.

Minimum requirement is to slaughter two or three hens and to prepare some *t'äla* (beer) or *qäribo* (unfermented beer). One of the hens is to be given to "the people" and the rest consumed ritually in the house. Ebrahim explains that the cost of the ritual is an obstacle that makes it hard to fulfil this tradition of the forefathers:

"We used to make it, but now we have stopped because when the right time is there, we do not have the capacity to buy the necessary items. We will think that we can make it next year, but when the time is there again, we meet the same problem. We used to make it in April, but now we do not arrange *mäwäkäl* any more."

In April this year, however, the impression of Hasän and Kadija's household as the economically strongest among the neighbours is strengthened by the fact that preparations start for a *mäwäkäl* for Hasän.

Also the preparations need careful consideration. Hasän is very concerned with finding the right day to buy the necessary items. The date is set to 27 *Miyazya* (5 May). Since a contagious disease flourishes among the hen population in the area, Hasän had wanted to buy the hens the day before the ceremony, on Monday. But as it rained the night before the preceding Wednesday, he orders Kadija to purchase the hens that day. I get no explanation why it is the correct day to buy the hens – perhaps it is connected with the purpose of the ritual – to thank Allah for answering the prayers – and the strongest prayers must have been to let Him bring rain, for long now. The hens for Hasän's *mäwäkäl* have to be red and white.

People are happy for the rain. It has already rained quite a lot in Kombolcha, and now it has finally reached Gäta, too. Now it is meaningful to sow, and if the weather remains good, there will be no food problem in September-October.

The preparations for Hasän's *mäwäkäl* start early in the morning of 27 *Miayazya*. The ritual slaughter of the hens, two red and a white one, has to be done by Hasän himself, and everybody who is to participate in the following ceremony has to be present by then. It will not be possible to enter the house where the ritual takes place after the hens are slaughtered. That is dangerous, it will cause harm on Hasän as well as the others.

At 8.30 a.m. everybody is in Hasän's house. Women and children are situated on the small platform in one corner, while the men sit behind a curtain in the centre of the house. Hasän's sons Säyäd and Ebrahim are there, and Ebrahim Shéhu and Mähamäd Ahmäd (Fat'é's son – this is his first time to participate as a grown man in such a ritual). Apart from Tolosa and myself, there are only two men who do not belong to the group of close relatives. They are learned men, and friends of Hasän, *Shéh* Säyäd, and Ahmäd Muhé. *Shéh* Säyäd is the ceremonial master, the *abägar*. Hasän first asked Ebrahim *Shéh*u to act as his ceremonial master, but both Ebrahim and Amu insisted that it had to be someone closer to Hasän's own age.

A curtain also covers the entrance to the house, and another is used to make a secluded room outside the house, in which the hens are to be slaughtered. Hasän's sons are with him, they go in and out of the house, ask the women for knives; the first one is rejected and another one is sharpened before it is sent out. In the meantime, bread is cut by Ebrahim Shéhu and returned to the women, who distribute it to the children. Kadija also assists her husband with the slaughtering. She goes in and out, brings water, and brings the slaughtered hens one by one back into the house, where they are left on the edge of the women's platform for some time, before they are taken away by the other women who start the preparations to cook them.

Women and children at Hasän's mäwäkäl

Kadija also brings butter, and she asks *Shéh* Säyäd if she can anoint it on the men's heads now. The *Shéh* says it can wait, but the women disagree, this is *mäwäkäl* they say and it has to be done now. Hasän instructs her that it is enough to distribute it only to a few of the men, and she smears it on the foreheads of the *Shéh* and Mähamäd.

More bread is brought to Ebrahim, who breaks it this time and places it on a small *mäsob* (a round footed basket made of coloured straws, used for serving food). A bowl with a *tälba* (flax) and water mixture is placed in the middle. Red pepper (*bärbäré*) is added to the liquid and we eat the bread after dipping it in the peppered flax mixture. The room, filled with people sitting on mats and cowhides on the floor, smells strongly of goat, as the goats spend the nights there with their owners. The bread has a strong, sour taste, and goes well with the milder flax solution (which also becomes stronger after a second round of *bärbäré* is added – Säyäd Hasän insists). After the bread *qäribo* is served, with a thick layer of bits and pieces of straws and other solid remains of the raw materials used in the brewing process floating on top in the gourd. The women roast *qolo* – a variety of grain – and serve it to everybody present. Then coffee is served, with more ceremony than usual. Hasän's son Ebrahim is the *kädami*, the one who serves the coffee. He stands while *Shéh* Säyäd chants his blessings; all the others follow him, hands turned up with open palms, chanting *"amèn, amèn"*. Smoke from incense and fragrant wood chips (*sändäl*) adds to the atmosphere in the room.

Hasän at his mäwäkäl

Now the religious content of the ceremony comes to the forefront, and *Shéh* Säyäd gets everybody's attention. He addresses Hasän, and tells him that he is very lucky, since his *mäwäkäl* falls on the *Ashura* – the Muslim New Year. "Allah tells us that this is *Ashura*, the time for changing year and for other changes," the *shéh* says. I ask him what year we now have reached in the Muslim calendar: "It is the same [as ours], but it is possible that there is a particular number in Arabic, but I don't know it. It is the same with *sharia* — some people think that *sharia* law is different, but it is the same, there is no difference. *Sera and näw* (it works the same way)". Later he comes back to the topic, and tells us that according to the Koran, it is about 500 years since the Muslim calendar started.

The role of the *shéh* is not only to officiate in the ceremonial parts of the ritual – he is also the educator and religious guide, and he tells a row of parables, that serve to guide his listeners about good and bad behaviour.

At around 11 a.m. a bundle of *ch'at* is laid in front of the *shéh* and he starts his prayers, which gradually change into a singing chant, in which the other men join in unison. All of them have powerful and pleasant voices, and as the song goes on, it adds to the solemnity of the occasion. Meanwhile the *shéh* has shared the *ch'at* bundle in equal heaps, and Ebrahim Hasän has distributed it to each of the men. Most of them hold a leaf or two between their hands while they sing, sitting on the floor, swaying rhythmically from side to side, seemingly lost in the song. The singing lasts for about ten minutes, and again the *shéh* recites two prayers; Ebrahim Hasän, the *kädami*, standing, the others sitting, with hands lifted, open palms upwards, "*amén, amén*".

Much of the prayers are in Arabic, most probably the same prayers that are commonly used at the *mäwlid* festival (the celebration of Mohammed's birthday) — the major religious event in Gäta.

37

The *ch'at* is distributed during the chanting prayers and songs, but no one starts chewing before the prayers are over. Then the atmosphere becomes more relaxed and informal, but strongly influenced by the *shéh* who tells anecdotes and parables. As the *ch'at* chewing starts to give effect, some of the men become more excited, the occasional prayers and blessings are more intense, and even more so the replies ("*amén! amén!*).

Food is served, the hens cooked in a thin peppered sauce and *enjära*. Hasän is served separately from a pot where his food is made. Immediately after the food, another round of sweet, strong coffee is served, accompanied by incense. More prayers and songs follow, again from the *mäwlid* repertoire.

Hasän seems more composed than the others, but he follows the rhythm of the prayers and the songs, sitting on the floor with closed eyes and open palms. The whole ceremony is for him, and the old man, who usually likes to present himself as rather careless about much of what others respect and fear, is obviously deeply touched by the present occasion.

Hasän remains in seclusion also the day after the *mäwäkäl*. Only those of us who participated in the whole ritual the day before can see him, or be seen by him. The ritual the day before was made for his parents, from whom he "inherited" the custom, like his sons will do it for him when he is gone. The prayers, like the ritual, are about health, wealth, peace and love – among parents, in families, among people. Hasän has felt sick for some time. "I was depressed and felt a pain in my neck and back, as if I was carrying a heavy load. But since yesterday I have felt fine, it has gone now," he says.

Zänäba and Hasän at his mäwäkäl

Markets And Marketing

The people in Gäta actively use four markets in walking distance: Kombolcha, Adamé, Ancharo, and Harbu. Kombolcha is the large urban market, with two market days: the

38

major one on Saturdays, and the minor on Wednesdays. Adamé is a rural market that gathers people from all directions every Thursday. Ancharo is the other rural market, and the smallest among the four. Ancharo operates on Mondays. Harbu market lies close to the main road in Harbu town. Like Kombolcha, it operates on Saturdays. Harbu seems to be the least interesting market for the Gäta people, perhaps because of the distance and because Kombolcha is a better option.

The markets are colourful and lively views on market days, so different from the desolate, untidy space of unused marketplaces. At first sight, the markets seem almost to have appeared as spontaneous gatherings of buyers and sellers, animals and vegetables, women, men and children. Sellers sit with their merchandise in front of them, grain, pulses, vegetables or chickens; haggling with potential buyers who move around to check prices and qualities before arriving at a deal. But a closer look at any market will soon reveal that there is an internal logic and structure to it. The same kind of goods are sold at specific places in the market, so that sellers of coffee line up in one section, followed by coffee bean husk sellers, surrounded by sections for spices and incense. Grain one place, pulses another. Petty traders with only a few kilograms of one or two products sit around the bigger traders who carry with them large sacks of grain, coffee, or spices, and who occupy more permanent selling stands, protected from sun or rain by canvas and plastic covers on top of wooden frames. Artisan work, like clay work and metal work, is always found at the perimeters of the marketplace, mirroring the ambiguous status of the craftsmen and their products as useful and dangerous at the same time, usually expressed as *buda*, their alleged inherent power of the evil eye. All the sellers, I was told, are taxed by the municipality and even the most unassuming petty trader has to pay one birr for the spot she or he occupies. The fee of one birr per market day is collected from the traders by people who are assigned by the municipality.

Most markets are surrounded by more permanent places for trade and commerce: shops, stores, and houses where refreshments are sold. In Kombolcha, all of these are present, and particularly the big concrete stores and the large hall for indoor shops are visual marks of the large marketplace. Kombolcha is a place for trade of all levels of quantity and sophistication, where large numbers of peasants dealing with handfuls of onions or grain mingle with professional and semi-professional traders who deal with truckloads rather than *ch'enät* (donkey loads) or *sahen* and *wälo* (plates and cups). The hierarchy of trade is complex and fascinating, both in terms of the many hands a transaction passes through before it finally ends up with a consumer, and in terms of markets. All the four households in Gäta are involved in petty trade. Their profit margin lies in the price difference of items at different markets. The Adamé market attracts peasants from the lower tracts to the east, most of them, it seems to me, selling their own products. There is also a rather big section in the market with butter trade, where there seems to be a mix of producers and traders who are selling. Small traders buy from them and bring it to the bigger markets where it is sold at a slightly higher price. So also with onions, garlic, eggs, vegetables, spices, oilseeds, sugarcanes, and grain. The Gäta women, like Kadija and Zämu, usually buy small quantities of onion and garlic at the urban Kombolcha market and sell it in Adamé. The small price difference they may achieve is counted as profit – the value of their time spent (two days work) is not counted.

Butter sellers in Adamé

Fat'é's house is probably the one which is presently least active in petty trade, due to lack of cash and of things to sell. But she also has to buy from the market. Her son Mahämäd went, as mentioned, to Kombolcha to sell *zängäda* stalks, but they also principally depend on the market to buy sugar and salt, soap, and household utensils. The market for them is just a degree more advanced than direct barter – *zängada* stalks sold for birr 2.50, salt and *gwaya* bought for birr 2.60. The Gäta people have little or no experience with the rest of the town; they never go shopping in the streets and have never set foot in a restaurant or coffee house – at least not the women. Kadija, in her high age, and Zämu, were both introduced to *läslasa* – softdrinks – for the first time in their lives when I invited them to one of the simple cafés at the entrance of the Kombolcha market. They were not comfortable at the table, but marvelled over the sparkling Fanta they drank, most probably only to please me, who had insisted on buying such a costly drink for them.

Kadija selling onions in Adamé

40

Kadija is the trader in Hasän's house; her son Ebrahim assists sometimes. Amu is not strong enough to walk long distances, so Zämu is the trader in her house. Like in the other households, it is the man, Ebrahim, who deals with buying and selling animals, while petty trade with onions and grain is women's work. Fat'ima and Säyäd are slightly more advanced traders than the others. Fat'ima has invested a loan she received through a credit scheme for rural women in grain, bought at the Adamé market and sold at Kombolcha. Säyäd assists her with transportation, and perhaps also marketing. The first round of trade was at least not a loss and probably even slightly profitable. Fat'ima received 300 birr from the credit scheme for women that was run by the Irish NGO *Concern*. She invested it in grain to trade with and paid back the loan "from the profit", she says. Now the credit scheme is open also for men, but it is still in Fat'ima's name that she and Säyäd borrow money. Fat'ima has now borrowed more money, 500 birr, and she has problems with getting the *aja* (oats) sold in Kombolcha without a loss. She has problems paying back the loan when the oats price in the market is so low, probably because there are too many sellers of oats at present. Several market days pass with hardly any sales. In mid-May Fat'ima tries her luck again, by buying *aja* for 50 birr at a rate of 2 birr for 4 *wälo* (as against two for five a couple of weeks earlier). Säyäd disapprovingly tells her what she seems to realise herself: "This is too expensive, you shouldn't have bought now." A couple of days later she again tries to sell her *aja* in Kombolcha, but there are no customers at all. The day after she has to borrow money from somebody to pay her weekly amount, 11.80 birr, to the credit association. A woman in Ch'aqorti is the elected leader of the association. She collects the weekly instalments from the members and deposits the money in a bank account in Kombolcha. Debt is a common, and feared, companion of the poor in Gäta, and particularly debt to the government, which Fat'ima in reality has incurred by borrowing from the credit scheme.

In April-May 1998 reserves are drying up and the markets are full of people who try to make at least a small amount of money by selling small quantities of grain, vegetables, or animals. One day at the Ancharo market, I stop and talk with a small group of people who sit close to a tiny heap of *t'éf* grain. It is an elderly couple and their daughter who explain that they have come to the market with this little amount of grain from their own product, to try and sell it. There seems to be hundreds of people doing the same, patiently waiting in long rows for customers to stop and buy from them.

At least two connected factors contribute to the swelling of the markets by sellers and the conspicuous lack of interested buyers: the lack of food, money and also seeds, and more than plenty of time available, since there is hardly any sensible agricultural work. It seems that all are bound to lose, both sellers and buyers, except the biggest traders who have enough capital to sustain periodic losses and to wait until better bargains can be made again. But all traders are on the outlook for price differences, to buy at one market and sell at another, where the unit price is slightly higher. It is almost a lottery, but the traders know the regularities: where things typically are cheaper, where the best qualities are found, and the value in the relationship between days and places. For example, it seems to be well established that prices are generally higher on Wednesdays in Kombolcha (the minor market day) compared to Saturdays (the major market day), and that the best market for animals, in terms of possibilities both to sell and buy, is the one in

Ancharo. Zämu trades mainly with onions and garlic. She buys in Kombolcha and sells in Adamé, and she estimates that she can make a profit of 3-4 birr per plastic dish *(sahen)* of garlic.

Fat'ima's husband Säyäd bought two sacks *(kächa)* of oats at the Adamé market in mid-April, and Fat'ima tries to sell it in Kombolcha (and occasionally in Harbu), but it takes weeks. Presently she says, "I try only to get back what I paid for it myself in Adamé." She explains that the oats were bought in Adamé for 2 birr per five *wälo* (small tin boxes). She now sells the oats for 1.70 birr per *sahen* (a plastic plate). Furthermore, one *sahen* is equal to five *wälo*. When I ask her if this is not selling at a loss, she says it would have been good to sell at 2 birr, but she cannot expect profit now. We do not quite agree on whether she covers her expenses (as she seems to say) or, as I calculate, she looses money by each transaction (30 cents per *sahen*). Perhaps there is a profit margin in the measurement units, *wälo* in Adamé, *sahen* in Kombolcha (to make matters of small scale trade more complicated, one *martin* is equal to two *timatim wälo*). But the expenditures in addition to the buying price are also in disfavour of a profitable account. She keeps the sack in the store that belongs to a trader in Kombolcha and pays 25 cents a week for the storage. Her own transport up to Kombolcha and back costs 1.50 to 2.00 birr in each direction. Even if she does not sell anything, she has expenses amounting to at least 4.25 birr (market fee 1.00 birr, transport 3.00 birr, storage 0.25 birr). The cost of labour is not included. Few able-bodied persons would accept to work for others for a full day for anything less than 5-10 birr. The value of one's own time is usually not calculated in monetary terms. The women have no other expenses; they sit the whole day at the market without food or drink. Men who have business at the market are more inclined to spend some money on a few drinks, at least to wet a deal *(fit'är)* when an animal has changed owner at the rural markets of Adamé or Ancharo. The drinking houses may have both the alcoholic *t'äla* beer and its unfermented cousin *qäribo*, which is similar to *t'äla* but without the hop-like brewing agent *gésho*. *Qäribo* can legally be drunk by Muslims because it is non (or low-) alcoholic, and it is, like *t'äla* among Christians, a drink for festive occasions and holidays. In the *t'äla* house at the perimeter of the Adamé market, the *t'äla* and the *qäribo* is served in big cups made of gourds, called *shekena*. In Ancharo the *t'äla* house is perhaps more modern: There the brew is served in *timatim* (literally "tomato"; ½ litre tomato paste tin boxes). The drinks are refreshing if they are well prepared and served at the right time. The inexperienced *t'äla* drinker will have some difficulties with fragments of the ingredients floating in the drink – to sieve out the biggest pieces while drinking and spitting them out inconspicuously requires some training.

The Adamé market lies south of Gäta, in a slightly sloping landscape with large plains and relatively small rocks. The market is accessible by car from Harbu town, but for my purpose it is necessary to walk with the Gäta people on the tracks they usually follow when they visit the market. We went on a sunny Thursday in late April 1998, with Ebrahim as our guide and companion. We did not set out from Gäta before 9 a.m. At that time, Kadija and Hasän had already left, and so had their son Ebrahim and Zämu, the daughter of Amu and Ebrahim.

42

The sun was not yet very strong, and the road was gentle. After the first, rather sharp, downhill stretch, the path stretched out on a wide plain, cracking dry at this time, with flocks of grazing cattle here and there, and beyond that little activity. As we approached the market, which lies on a small and stony hill at the other side of the big plain, we saw seemingly endless rows of people walking towards the same destination. Many carried sacks of products to be sold at the market, and some used donkeys to carry their loads. Many had walked for hours since early in the morning and had a steady and economic pace, unaffected by the gradual rise of the path. Ebrahim met many acquaintances, which quite naturally were curious about the strangers in his company. Proudly he told them that we were his friends, and that we came on foot from Gäta, a very peculiar thing to do, it seemed, for people of our kind, and particularly for a *färänj* – a white man. This fact made Ebrahim even prouder, and he made us speed up as if to demonstrate how strong "his" *färänj* was. Consequently, we were both thirsty and tired when we arrived at the bustling market after a one and half hours walk. The following day Amu laughingly told us that the journey had been too demanding for Ebrahim, he was sick and had to keep to the bed. From the spark in her eyes, it seemed that Amu liked the idea of having a husband who, despite his age, liked to show off his strength when travelling with others.

Adamé was similar to other rural markets in Wälo; well organised, different items sold at different places of the market, cattle and pottery in the outskirts, and small traders in rows together with others trading the same products. The marketplace was quite hilly and stony and very crowded, making it difficult to move around. A *färänj* with a camera obviously evokes people's curiosity, and I was approached by a young man, probably a cadre or some official. Stuttering in a barely understandable English he explained to me that "the people" had asked him to find out what I did and what I wanted, more specifically if I came to start another assistance programme – there was a big need for assistance since there were many leprosy victims. He pretended to accept my explanation that I was only there to look and that I had no attachment to any NGOs, but many people asked me during the day if it was really true that I did not work for Concern – the NGO that had operated in the area previously.

A particular feature with the Adamé market is the many butter sellers. Rows of women, of a darker complexion than the Gäta people, sold butter from simple containers to consumers and to middlemen (and women). Most of them had small balance scales, using batteries of different size as the unit weight. According to Ebrahim, the butter-selling women are Muslim Amharas from the lowland (to the east), where the economy probably is much more geared towards pastoralism than in the highlands.

We met both Kadija and Zämu at the market, each with their small heaps of onion and garlic which they had bought earlier at the market in Kombolcha. Kadija, at least, had sold all that she brought with her, she told us the following day. Zämu was also satisfied with her trade, and the next day she showed us a brand new coffee tray (*räkabot*) that she had bought there.

The sun and dust made us thirsty, and we started searching for a place to buy something to drink. We found a house where dark, sweet tea was sold, and later, before leaving the market, Hasän and Ebrahim took us to a house where *t'äla* and *karibo* was sold, at a price of 60 cents per gourd (*shekena*). As we started our return journey, Hasän picked up a heifer he had bought earlier. He told us that it was not for himself, but for his daughter Zänäba, who lived in Kombolcha. She had given her father money that she had earned from another transaction she had made earlier: She had bought a small goat kid for 7 birr, and her father kept it for her until it had grown fat, and sold it during the Muslim festival of *aräfa* for 280 birr. Hasän now had paid 245 birr for the heifer. Now the heifer would be kept by Hasän and his family and hopefully give Zänäba more income. "It is not *rebi*," Hasän explained, "because Zänäba is my daughter I do it for her. But we will use the milk. When I die, Zänäba will even have a claim on my other animals".

Ebrahim drinks qaribo *in the Anchäro market*

Property Rights

Much has happened with property rights, particularly land rights, since the revolution in 1974 and the Land Reform of the new revolutionary government, the *Därg*, in 1975. Hasän, or his father, had much land before the revolution. Some of the land had been in the family for generations, while parts of it had been given to Hasän's paternal grandfather by the Emperor, for services to the crown. Hasän was born on the opposite (western) side of Borkana river. In Hasän's father's time, land estates were measured in "shields" (*gasha*) – one *gasha* is normally estimated to be about 40 ha. The land was called *gäbar märét*; Hasän's father had half a "shield" of that. In addition he had inherited his father's ¼ "shield" of *yä-galla märét* – literally in today's language "Oromo land", but it does not necessarily have to do with Oromos, it simply means government land (Hasän also translates it with *yä-mängest märét*). "The only difference between the two types of land," explains Hasän, "was the tax on the land."

The family lost all this land after the revolution. It was located in different *qäbälés* and Hasän had nothing in the *qäbälé* where they lived. "This was the policy, there was nothing to do about it. So I only got my share in the distribution of land."

Hasän's grandfather, Wäraqé, served as a *ch'iqa shum* for a long time. The *ch'iqa shum* was the lowest official in the government hierarchy before the revolution and served as the village headman. This official was, among other things, responsible for collecting taxes. Wäräqé's son Mariyé, Hasän's father, also had this position for some time, probably until the Italian occupation. "The *Galla märét* was given by the Emperor to soldiers that had served him," Hasän explains, "you could use it as long as you lived, but it always belonged to the state. But the land could be inherited – once it was given, it could not be taken back because it could be inherited by the children. But the *balabat* would have their own share in it." Hasän says that this system stopped at the arrival of the "foreigners" (*färanjoch*; in this context, the Italian occupation): "Since the *färanjoch* came, these arrangements stopped and government employees were paid only salaries, and got no remuneration in the form of land. Nowadays all land belongs to the state; government servants (*ashkär*) now only get their salary."

Hasän was a member of the first land distribution committee in the Peasant Association, just after the revolution. The work was completed after one and a half years, and the committee was dissolved. "When we measured the land, we took land from people with much land in relation to the number of household members, and gave to people with little land," he explains. It seems that in Gäta, the normal rule was to give one *t'emad* of land per household member.

The land Hasän and Ebrahim Shehu now plough was land that Kadija and Ebrahim inherited from their mothers, who in turn had inherited it from their father. In Gäta, it was commonly said that "women do not inherit land". This must not be taken literally, in other cases it was stressed that daughters had the same inheritance rights in the family property as sons. Kadija explains that in practice, however, a daughter who marries someone with land and moves to him will not have a claim on her share of the family land. This is also practised today. In this particular case, the inheritance eventually went through three women. Ahmäd Hasän was the inheritor of his father Hasän Särach, the great grandfather of Kadija and Ebrahim. When Ahmäd Hasän died, his sisters Bäyänäch Hasän (Kadija's mother) and Aminat Hasän, Ebrahim's mother, were the inheritors. Ebrahim was the only surviving child of Aminat and kept the land. In Bäyänäch's case, her land was first inherited by her son Ahmäd. Her other son also got his share, but for many years he never claimed it. He worked for the Italians, and moved with them to Tegray, and the family did not hear from him for many years. When he finally came home, he decided to decline his inheritance and migrated to Däsé, where he was employed by the Ethiopian Telecommunication Company. As he did this, he passed the right to the land to his sister Kadija. Ahmäd's land was inherited by his daughter, but since she lived in the town at the time of the land reform and the following land distribution, she lost her claim. From Kadija's story, it seems that she also took over this land.

Some of Ebrahim's land was included in the neighbouring *qäbälé*, Baké, at the time of the distribution (at that time, the administrative borders were changed and some land fell at the other side of the new *qäbälé* borders). The land reform regulations of 1975 prohibited land ownership by non-residents of the *qäbälé* where the land was, so Ebrahim lost his land which now was in Baké. He kept the land that was within the borders of Ch'orisa *qäbälé*, probably since it was measured to 5 *t'emad*, corresponding to the number of household members at that time. The *t'emad* is a flexible measurement unit that can accommodate other dimensions than the spatial extension, like quality of the soil, work input, and, in the context of equity, social and political considerations.

Ebrahim also served the *qäbälé* immediately after the revolution. He was a member of the local militia for two years, during the time of the land redistribution (1967-68 E.C.) "The land was taken from the rich and given to the poor," he says, "but without any real measurements. The actual measurements were made one year after, in 1969 (E.C.)."

Kadija tells the story of the land in a slightly different version compared to Hasän and Ebrahim. She tells that before the revolution, she was the sole owner of the land that she had inherited from her mother's father, including the land Ebrahim later received at the land distribution. Kadija too, lost land to Baké. "I inherited the land from my mother's father," she says, "and he had also inherited it. When land is inherited generation by generation, it is called *bä-wers*" (literally "by inheritance"). The land Kadija inherited has now in practice been transferred to her and Hasän's sons Säyäd and Ebrahim.

Women do normally relinquish their right to their share of their family's land if they marry and move out. Hasän explained the rationale of this as follows: "Because my daughters are married and have moved out, my sons will share the father-land. My daughters have the right to share other inheritance, like money, but they are not entitled to the land. The land becomes very small as time goes. It is like slaughtering an ox – if the whole animal is for one family it is more than enough, but if it is shared by forty people, it is only one meal for each of them." In fact, this does not only apply to women. A son who moves out, like Kadija's brother, also usually refrains from his rights to the land, leaving it to the remaining relatives. Residence and occupation, more than sex, decides who in practice inherits the land.

Amu, who many times demonstrates a sharp and uncensored intellect with an eye for unreasonable social or cultural "facts", comments that Hasän's sons most probably will block their sister from her rightful share of the inheritance – this is probably what many women experience when the time for sharing with male relatives comes. Hasän protests, "that is impossible," he says, "but she cannot inherit land because she has her own share where she is – she was not a member of this household at the time of the land distribution and therefore she has no claim to the land of the household." This probably refers to one of the daughters who had moved out and married before the land reform, and therefore received land as a member of that household. My guess is that this is Aysha, who lives in a nearby *qäbälé* with her husband and children.

46

Zänäba and Abdi: The Townspeople

Zänäba is the oldest surviving child of Kadija and Hasän. Her older sister died a year after she had her first child, a girl, and her husband died soon after. I do not know if they were survived by their daughter, but today the entire little family is gone. Zänäba's two younger sisters live in rural areas not far from Gäta. The older one, Aisha, is married and has many children, while the youngest, Zänit, is married but without children. None of them seem to visit their parents as often as Zänäba. Kadija meets her daughter frequently in connection with her petty trade in Kombolcha, while Hasän does not feel strong enough to move with any frequency from Gäta. Sometimes, though, he will visit Aisha and her family who live very close. Zänäba's "uncle", Ebrahim Shéhu, remembers that she was four years old when he first married, 34 years ago. Zänäba is a sympathetic woman who does not attempt to hide her affection for her little family or the fondness she has for her parents and brothers and the rest of the little community in Gäta. The love is mutual, and whenever Zänäba and her daughters pay a visit, the atmosphere brightens up, and especially old Hasän, Zänäba's father, becomes reinvigorated and amicable in their company.

Abdi Muhé, Zänäba's husband, is a strong and sturdy man, about forty years old, his hair and beard speckled with grey. His steady and serious look hides a humorous and loving character; qualities which temper the worries and frustrations that otherwise would have broken out in full rage. Abdi and Zänäba are the most important link for their relatives in Gäta to the urban services in Kombolcha. They have lived together for a long time as urban dwellers, first in the Eritrean port Asäb and later, after Ethiopian citizens were dispelled from Eritrea, in the crowded living quarters of Kombolcha.

Abdi is Zänäba's second husband. She stayed with her first husband only for about half a year before she divorced him. Abdi was also married, and divorced his first wife at the same time as Zänäba left her husband. Neither of them had children in their first marriage. Their first child, a boy, was born more than ten years after they married, just after the EPRDF take-over in 1991. It is unusual for couples to live together so long without children. Most rural marriages will be dissolved if childless, because children are needed as additional hands in the work and as a substitute for pension schemes in old age. That Abdi and Zänäba kept together despite the lack of children is perhaps explained by the fact that they lived in Asäb for more than ten years, where Abdi, like Fat'é's husband, worked as a labourer in the port. The urban life was probably more adjustable to barrenness than a rural context would have been. Still, there is a certain shine of something special and valuable that surrounds the biography of their married life; it seems so unusual that they have been living together in genuine "twosomeness" for so long. The dyad, so highly valued and celebrated in Western society, is a rare thing in Ethiopia and particularly in the countryside. But Zänäba and Abdi also had their rows and disagreements, and Abdi once sent her away from Asäb, home to her parents. The story about how she found her way back to Asäb; to find work, perhaps, or to reconcile with Abdi, is both sweet and romantic as they finally reunited and continued their married life together.

Abdi worked for *Bahr Transport* (*bahr* is Amharic for sea or ocean), a government company with more than 3,000 employees. Hard manual work gave relatively good incomes for the labourers. Abdi and his friends from Asäb, who now live in the same quarter in Kombolcha, recall how hard they worked to unload the ships that came with grain from donor countries in *säbasäbat*, during the drought and famine in 1984/85. They worked almost day and night, making it a sport to compete among themselves and get the life-giving food off the ships and over to trucks. Their narrative is engaging and lively, until a strike of bitterness enters into it, when they come to the point in their story where they deal with government officials and other persons of authority who misused their positions to make fortunes out of the food that was meant for the famished population. A large proportion of the food aid was stolen already in the harbour, they say. Very little reached the famine victims. And they recall the loads of grain that were arrested on board the ships while the donors and the military government haggled over the issue of port fees and import taxes which the government imposed on the aid. At the same time, people were employed in Harbu town to dig graves for famine victims that could not be helped by the relief operation there.

Apart from this grim period, life in Asäb seems to have been hard but with a sparkling optimism. In early 1991, Abdi and Zänäba expected their first child, and they were investing their money in a house of their own. Most of the house was finished, equipment and furniture were bought and fees for electricity and water had been paid, when everything was lost in a dramatic stroke. Ethiopia had been liberated from the hated military regime, Mengistu Haile Mariam had fled from the country, and the Tigrayan People's Liberation Front (TPLF) forces had taken over Addis Ababa. It was only a matter of time and formalities before the northern province Eritrea, which now was controlled by the Eritrean People's Liberation Front (EPLF), was to become an independent state. Ethiopian citizens at the best faced an uncertain future in a foreign country. For Zänäba and Abdi, however, the seriousness of the situation was immediate. Heavy fighting prior to the Därg's defeat made life difficult and uncertain, and the location of the living quarters close to the large oil refinery made them feel as if they were living on an enormous bomb that could blow up at any time. One direct hit from the Ethiopian MIG jets would have been enough. The workers made hurried decisions, and assisted by the authorities, they fled from Asäb towards Addis Ababa. Zänäba, late in her first pregnancy, left Asäb by road in May 1991 (18th *Genbot* 1983 E.C.). Abdi left with an organised boat transport to Djibouti two days later. They left everything behind them but saved their lives. In Addis Ababa, the displaced people from Eritrea were placed at a football field where they were given food and shelter by the new government. The Asäb workers argued for their right of a compensation from the government for the work they had done in Asäb, and for the things they had lost, but even a long hunger strike did not work in their favour. After 45 days at the football field in Addis Ababa, the hunger strike was called off, and people were dispersed to different corners of the country. Abdi and his displaced friends cannot hide their bitterness over the then prime minister of the transitional government, Tamrat Layne. The prime minister had argued against the striking refugees that the previous government had forced brothers and fathers to fight and that the army did not distinguish between soldiers and civilians, and that his new government did not distinguish between fighters and non-fighters. "You have fought against us," Abdi recalls Tamrat to have said, "so we don't owe you a compensation". The logic must have been that as Ethiopian workers in Asäb, they supported the Därg regime and worked against the Eritrean liberation fight. Whatever the reasons were, they will not be understood or accepted by the workers who ended up as refugees in their own country. "I have stopped registering what happened after we were displaced," Abdi says resignedly. "It is only God who can do that, it is too much for man."

Zänäba reached home to Gäta in time to give birth to her first child, and the boy was born in June 1991 (20ᵗʰ *Säné* 1983 E.C.). The boy died shortly after. Zänäba and Abdi's oldest daughter, Mädina, was born 14 months later, in August 1992 (25 *Nähasé* 1984 E.C.) Mädina's little sister, Sa'ada, is three years younger. She was born in July 1995 (3ʳᵈ *Hamlé* 1987 E.C.).

At the time when Mädina was born, sickness dominated the family. Zänäba was sick during her pregnancy, and Abdi says he does not remember the birth; he was almost unconscious at the time. He vomited blood, and Kadija stayed with the little family for months and cared for them. "After some time my friends came with *ch'at*, coffee, and sugar and made *du'a* for me," he recalls. "I tried to eat a little, but I avoided eating from our own house, the food came from neighbours. I stopped throwing up, but the same evening I became ill again. I decided to stop drinking cold water, I boiled water and drank it lukewarm – that is how I saved my life. I didn't drink cold water for the next five years, it is only four months since I started that again."

Mädina has got her name as a remembrance of the sickness in the family at the time she was born. A neighbour, commenting that the baby girl was born between two sick people, her mother and father, said that the girl is *mädhen* (lit. "immunity" or "saviour") – the saviour of her parents' lives – and consequently her name had to be Mädina.

The little family established themselves in Kombolcha, in a part of the town where many displaced persons from Eritrea live. The little community of displaced persons – Abdi says they are 160 living in Kombolcha – shrinks as members die, and some are perhaps moving out. Their common destiny keeps them together, trying to ease the hardships that befall them as urban poor. They are not formally organised, with the exception of the *yä-afär qiré* – the burial association. Abdi sees this as a bitter symbol of their situation – "the only purpose of the association," he says, "is to bury people when they die." The members who pay do not pay a regular fee for their membership just contribute to the costs and take responsibility for the funeral whenever a member dies. "There are many who don't have a family here, if they are not taken care of when they die they would be left to be eaten by the hyenas," is Abdi's harsh description of the desolate life of single returnees from Eritrea. Each member contributes 25 cents to the little ceremony after the funeral. It is only seven days since one of their neighbours died – he worked with Abdi in Asäb and they travelled back to Kombolcha together. When his children come and greet me, I cannot avoid thinking of how their future will look like. It seems bleak indeed.

Zänäba, Abdi and Mädina

Abdi's life seems to be very dependent on his immediate family – Zänäba, Mädina and Sa'ada – all his physical strength and emotional energy is directed towards their well being. He also is full of concern for his in-laws, Zänäba's conjugal family, and particularly his parents-in-law, Kadija and Hasän. Abdi seems to have no contact with his own conjugal family. Both his parents are dead, and he mentions only two sisters, one who lives in Bäké, not far from Gäta, the other in "Oromoland" in the south. He has not seen the latter sister for the last twenty years, he explains. "For people like me, without land of their own, there is only one opportunity, the petty trade at the market. Our relatives are not willing to share their land with us. But also the rural people do this: look at old Kadija, she buys onions here for 8 birr and take them to the Adamé market, where she can sell it with a profit of a few cents."

The room they rent in Kombolcha measures about 4 x 3 m. A big bed occupies much of the space, a couple of bamboo chairs and sacks of grain occupy most of the remaining floor, except for a small section of the floor which is covered with pieces of cloth, a typical feature of a Muslim home. Food, coffee, and *ch'at* are consumed sitting on the floor. Everybody takes the shoes off before sitting down at the simple cloth. The fleas, an unavoidable plague of urban and rural dwellings, tend to pester hosts and guests. A simple wooden cupboard serves to store cooking utensils and other small items. Cooking is done outdoors, on small charcoal burners; coffee is prepared on the floor inside. Five persons share this little space; for some time now, Zänäba's niece Zähara has been living with them, looking after the small girls while their parents are at the market. The gravel road just above the compound is one of the main traffic lines through the residential area, and the parents fear that their little girls can be knocked down by passing cars or horse carts (*gari*), which outnumber the "ordinary" taxis in Kombolcha.

Zänäba and Abdi pay 30 birr per month in rent, in addition to the cost of water, from the communal water post, and electricity. "It is too much for us," complains Abdi, it is not easy to make ends meet. The bags of pulses in the room are not the family's food store, but the capital of their little trade. "We only eat the profit from the trade," says Abdi, "2-3 cups per day. Sometimes, when trade is low, we are forced to eat from the capital, when there is no profit." The lentils and other pulses have to be rinsed before they are sold at the market, a very time-consuming and boring work. Normally, it is done by women, and sometimes also the female neighbours of Zänäba and Abdi give a hand. This work is done under time pressure.

Abdi has a good sense for numbers. He is very exact on dates, like the date of the exodus from Asäb, the birth dates of his children, and the like; he remembers costs of medicines spent on sick relatives years ago, and he calculates rapidly the difference between buying and selling prices related to his marketing. The lentils (*meser*) which Zänäba and Abdi have invested all their capital in, 750 birr, turns out to be difficult to sell with a profit. A week ago prices were good, 5 birr per kg. Many petty traders have invested in lentils since then, and prices are now down. Early May, when they bought 200 kg (1 *quintal*) lentils, they paid 360 kg per *quintal*. There are additional costs, for threshing, transport, and storage, and about 20% of the lentils are lost in the threshing.

"We bought the lentils in *quintal*," Abdi explains. "At the same time lentils were sold at the market at 6.10 birr per *goma*, which gives a price per 100 kg of 366 birr" (60 *goma* is 1 *quintal*). "Last week we sold for 5 birr per kg. Now we are offered 4.75, which is a net loss for us."

One of the biggest merchants at the Kombolcha market is *Haji* Awol Ali. He owns a huge storehouse – the *magazin* – in the market, in addition to two mills in Kombolcha and two somewhere else, and two buses. He charges a fee for smaller traders who want to use his scale to weigh their goods (1 birr/*quintal*), and he offers storage (1 birr/*quintal* per week). Many traders, among them Zänäba and Abdi, are waiting for better offers outside the *magazin*. The *Haji* consistently and calmly refuses to buy for anything more than 4.75 now. His buyers are probably in Mercato, the huge market in Addis Ababa, where he competes at a national scale, it is a risky business for him too. But he obviously has a much more solid economy, with capital that can absorb the shocks of occasional losses. For Zänäba and Abdi, this is a serious limitation. "Our capital is bound in these goods and if we don't sell we are stuck. People who bought lentils today can sell cheaper than us and the price can go further down, at least by 10% more," Abdi says, and he dryly adds, "I am not going to buy lentils again."

Zänäba with her lentils outside the magazin *in Kombolcha*

Postscript: Four Years Later

Since my one month long fieldwork in Gäta in 1998, I have revisited the little community in Gäta several times, usually only for a few days. My hitherto last visit was in May 2002. During the four years, seasons had come and gone, crops had sometimes failed and sometimes been good, cattle had been bought and sold, and some members of the little community had passed away and new ones had been born. Old Hasän died in October 1998. Less than a year after, Zänäba, his favourite daughter who lived in Kombolcha with her husband Abdi and their two daughters, also died, leaving Abdi and the girls in distress and deeper poverty than ever. Zähara, the oldest daughter of Säyäd, who for some time had been living in Kombolcha to look after her cousins, Zänäba's and Abdi's daughters, had for some time lived in Gäta, but in April 2001 she married a man living elsewhere in Ch'orisa *qäbälé*. I saw Muntaha, the old neighbour and relative, for the last time in October 2000. She was very weak, and when I entered her house to greet her, she could barely manage to get up from the bed she was sitting on. We greeted each other by ceremonial kisses, both of us conscious of the fact that this probably is the last time we meet. She died not long after, I was later told.

The household of Fat'é Hasän, the widow, has grown by two members. Her daughter Aysha has moved – temporarily perhaps – from her husband and lives in her mother's house. She also has her infant boy with her. The only man in Fat'é's house, her son Mähamäd, is now a fully grown man, at the height of his manly strength. He works harder than ever for the benefit of the little family. He is officially registered in the *qäbälé* taxlist as the owner of the land, because, as his mother says, he is better fitted to represent the household in matters of politics and communal labour. Some time back, Mähamäd had decided to give up agriculture and leave the area in search for paid work, a common outlet for the Wälo youngsters. His mother had begged him to stay, not to leave her and his sister alone on the land, and finally he was persuaded to stay, after strong appeals and night-long *du'a* ceremonies. It is still evident that the young man is full of energetic restlessness, trapped between loyalty to his ageing mother and a need to find a better life for himself.

Also Aysha Ebrahim, the oldest daughter of Amu and Ebrahim and Jämal's mother, has moved home to her parents' house. Her husband died just a few days after Zänäba in the rainy season (*kerämt*) of 2000. Zänäba had refrained from claiming her share from her husband's land (in Bäké *qäbälé*): "If I had taken the case to the court, I could have won. But I decided against it. He had three sons and a daughter, and only little land. We were five people left and the land was too small to be shared among us. It is more advantageous to be here [in her parents' household]".

Aysha also brought with her a baby, about one and a half years old. She was conceived when Aysha was raped on her way home from a food-for-work (FFW) site. Aysha had been assigned as the secretary at the site of the FFW project, and she was the last to leave in the evening. The young man had waited for her along the road. She knew him very well, his family was related to her deceased husband and they were also related to Amu, Aysha's mother. "He was almost a relative, and I didn't expect him to do this to me," Aysha says. "After I realised that I was pregnant, I informed him about it. He immediately sold his family's ox and went to Jimma. After several telephone calls to him, he finally acknowledged that he is the father. But he never sent anything to support us. (…) I could have presented this case to the court, but it would have been unsafe for my father. He is alone, and they [the rapist's family] could kill him. They have already harassed my father, fearing that we would take the case to court. So I leave it, it is better that I suffer as long as my father is unharmed." Rape and abuse are still common in the rural area. Amu commented: "Now women's rights are protected by the law, but still, this is only words, until now this is not practiced here, we do not have this experience, but we have heard that it is underway in the towns."

Abdi and his little family in Kombolcha were seriously troubled by Zänäba's death. A couple of times previous to Zänäba's illness and death, some of my colleagues and myself had assisted Abdi with some money in order to get his little trade business up and going again. He had been full of energy and certain that his capital would grow with his skilled trade. Zänäba's deteriorating health brutally crushed his hopes. He spent all his money, about 2000 birr, on medicines and medical care for Zänäba. It did not save her life, and now he was left alone, with two little girls and no assisting hand in the trade activities. When I met him some months after Zänäba's death, he was totally changed, as if grief and worries had added years to his age. No word was spoken at first, he only embraced me, tears rolling down his cheeks. He was full of worries for the future of his children, and spent all his days searching for daily labour contracts, usually with no luck. When we met, eight days had passed since last time he had had a day's work. The daily pay was 5 birr. He had changed residence, an even smaller room than they had rented before. The rent was 30 birr per month, but now he was 2 months behind. The landlord, who lived in the same compound, was also one of the Asab returnees, and had been kind enough not to ask for the rent. Abdi also has to pay a monthly fee for drinking water, 5 birr.

Abdi's relationship to his Gäta in-laws became strained and difficult after both Zänäba's father and Zänäba herself were gone. Abdi complained that his mother-in-law, Kadija, who previously had been a regular visitor in Zänäba and Abdi's house in Kombolcha, had not been seen after the completion of the seven days mourning ceremonies. The chain of mutual assistance was broken. Abdi was bitter, and felt that Kadija, the grandmother of his children, did not fulfil her responsibilities as a close relative. At least she could have visited them, he said.

In Gäta, the discussion among the relatives was sometimes heated when the topic of Abdi and his children came up. Most of them found it difficult to understand why Kadija had turned her back to her grandchildren. They also admitted they were ashamed because none of them had visited Abdi regularly. Only one of Zänäba's brothers–in-law, who is married with Zänäba's sister Aysha Hasan, had been a regular visitor after Zänäba died. Kadija, when she was confronted directly with questions why she did not visit Abdi, argued that as an old woman, she was the one to be visited, and Abdi had not been in Gäta. The others still insisted that she should be above such considerations and fulfil her duties as grandmother.

Abdi's own explanation was that since he had nothing to offer the Gäta people anymore, they were not interested in him.

Abdi and I met again in February 2002. The rainy season that year had been tough. Food prices went high, and Abdi had sold much of his personal belongings to get cash for food and clothes for the children. 12 tea glasses, that they had brought with them from Asäb, a metal box that had been used to store clothes, a metal coffee pot, three of Zänäba's clothes, his own jacket; everything was sold. "I do not need any suitcase or clothes box," Abdi said, "I have nothing left. I decided to leave Kombolcha and travel to Addis Ababa to beg, but people gathered here and convinced me to stay and wait for things to get better."

Wood prices had also increased, a bundle of wood costs 15 birr. Abdi had paid a woman in the neighbourhood to make *enjära*, but later on a woman, Säyädu from Ch'orisa *qäbälé*, had joined him as his new wife. It was his landlord who had introduced him to Säyädu.

Säyädu had lived with the little family for some time but had decided to return to her own place again. When I visited Abdi in February 2002, she came back again. She was also distressed by the situation:

"I know that Abdi is hard working, he behaves well and doesn't waste money on *ch'at* or alcohol. The problem is lack of work. The children do not understand this; they think that I don't give them food because I don't want to, that I hide the *enjära* for them. Therefore I was torn between two decisions, and I decided to leave instead of being tormented like this. The children wanted to have *enjära*, and I had to look them into their eyes and tell them that there is nothing. I could see in their eyes that they thought I didn't give them because I am their stepmother."

54

When I left Abdi in February 2002, returning to my home country, he asked, as usual, when I would come back. I told him that the plan was to return to Ethiopia in June. I did spend a few nights in Kombolcha, in May, working in Ch'orisa and Gäta, before proceeding to North Wälo. I decided to visit Abdi when returning from the north, but when travelling back to Addis Ababa, time was too short to make a stop in Kombolcha. Consequently, we did not meet. In September 2002 a letter came to my address in Norway. The content of the letter, which somebody must have written for Abdi, since it was in English, was emotionally disturbing. Enclosed with it was a photograph that I had taken of Abdi and the girls some years ago.

In the letter he asked why I had not come to see him in June, as I had planned. Further, he wrote that he was sick: "I am becoming weaker and weaker. I have no work. I have nobody to support me. I always worry about my poor daughters' future life. You know that they don't have mother or any relative to help them. So, what do you think will their future life seem if I pass away? Street children?! I can't see any other chance." His letter ended with an appeal: "Dear Harald, these days I don't feel healthy. (...) hoping to get a good advice and solution, I am forced to write you this letter. So, please show me the bright future of my daughters while I am alive. Try to get them any organization to bring them up. I am very tired. Lend them your hand before I pass away."

FSS PUBLICATIONS LIST

FSS Newsletter

Medrek (Quarterly since 1998. English and Amharic)

FSS Discussion Papers

No. 1. *Water Resource Development in Ethiopia: Issues of Sustainability and Participation.* Dessalegn Rahmato. June 1999
No. 2. *The City of Addis Ababa: Policy Options for the Governance and Management of a City with Multiple Identity.* Meheret Ayenew. December 1999
No. 3. *Listening to the Poor: A Study Based on Selected Rural and Urban Sites in Ethiopia.* Aklilu Kidanu and Dessalegn Rahmato. May 2000
No. 4. *Small-Scale Irrigation and Household Food Security. A Case Study from Central Ethiopia.* Fuad Adem. February 2001
No. 5. *Land Redistribution and Female-Headed Households.* By Yigremew Adal. November 2001
No. 6. *Environmental Impact of Development Policies in Peripheral Areas: The Case of Metekel, Northwest Ethiopia.* Wolde-Selassie Abbute. Forthcoming, 2001
No. 7. *The Environmental Impact of Small-scale Irrigation: A Case Study.* Fuad Adem. Forthcoming, 2001
No. 8. *Livelihood Insecurity Among Urban Households in Ethiopia.* Dessalegn Rahmato and Aklilu Kidanu. October 2002
No. 9. *Rural Poverty in Ethiopia: Household Case Studies from North Shewa.* Yared Amare. December 2002
No.10. *Rural Lands in Ethiopia: Issues, Evidences and Policy Response.* Tesfaye Teklu. May 2003
No.11. *Resettlement in Ethiopia: The Tragedy of Population Relocation in the 1980s..* Dessalegn Rahmato. June 2003

FSS Monograph Series

No. 1. *Survey of the Private Press in Ethiopia: 1991-1999.* Shimelis Bonsa. 2000
No. 2. *Environmental Change and State Policy in Ethiopia: Lessons from Past Experience.* Dessalegn Rahmato. 2001

FSS Conference Proceedings

1. *Issues in Rural Development. Proceedings of the Inaugural Workshop of the Forum for Social Studies, 18 September 1998.* Edited by Zenebework Taddesse. 2000
2. *Development and Public Access to Information in Ethiopia.* Edited by Zenebework Tadesse. 2000
3. *Environment and Development in Ethiopia.* Edited by Zenebework Tadesse. 2001
4. *Food Security and Sustainable Livelihoods in Ethiopia.* Edited by Yared Amare. 2001
5. *Natural Resource Management in Ethiopia.* Edited by Alula Pankhurst. 2001
6. *Poverty and Poverty Policy in Ethiopia.* Special issue containing the papers of FSS' final conference on poverty held on 8 March 2002

Consultation Papers on Poverty

No. 1.   *The Social Dimensions of Poverty.* Papers by Minas Hiruy, Abebe Kebede, and Zenebework Tadesse. Edited by Meheret Ayenew. June 2001

No. 2.   *NGOs and Poverty Reduction.* Papers by Fassil W. Mariam, Abowork Haile, Berhanu Geleto, and Jemal Ahmed. Edited by Meheret Ayenew. July 2001

No. 3.   *Civil Society Groups and Poverty Reduction.* Papers by Abonesh H. Mariam, Zena Berhanu, and Zewdie Shitie. Edited by Meheret Ayenew. August 2001

No. 4.   *Listening to the Poor.* Oral Presentation by Gizachew Haile, Senait Zenawi, Sisay Gessesse and Martha Tadesse. In Amharic. Edited by Meheret Ayenew. November 2001

No.5.   *The Private Sector and Poverty Reduction [Amharic].* Papers by Teshome Kebede, Mullu Solomon and Hailemeskel Abebe. Edited by Meheret Ayenew, November 2001

No.6.   *Government, Donors and Poverty Reduction.* Papers by H.E. Ato Mekonnen Manyazewal, William James Smith and Jeroen Verheul. Edited by Meheret Ayenew, February 2002.

No.7.   *Poverty and Poverty Policy in Ethiopia.* Edited by Meheret Ayenew, 2002

Books

1.   *Ethiopia: The Challenge of Democracy from Below.* Edited by Bahru Zewde and Siegfried Pausewang. Nordic African Institute, Uppsala and the Forum for Social Studies, Addis Ababa. 2002

Special Publications

Thematic Briefings on Natural Resource Management, Enlarged Edition. Edited by Alula Pankhurst. Produced jointly by the Forum for Social Studies and the University of Sussex. January 2001

New Series

• Gender Policy Dialogue Series

No. 1   *Gender and Economic Policy.* Edited by Zenebework Tadesse. March 2003
No. 2   *Gender and Poverty (Amharic).* Edited by Zenebework Tadese. March 2003

• Consultation Papers on Environment

No. 1   *Environment and Environmental Change in Ethiopia.* Edited by Gedion Asfaw. Consultation Papers on Environment. March 2003

No. 2   *Environment, Poverty and Gender.* Edited by Gedion Asfaw. Consultation Papers on Environment. May 2003

No. 3   *Environmental Conflict.* Edited by Gedion Asfaw. Consultation Papers on Environment. July 2003

• FSS Studies on Poverty

No. 1   *Some Aspects of Poverty in Ethiopia: Three Selected Papers.* Papers by Dessalegn Rahmato, Meheret Ayenew and Aklilu Kidanu. Edited by Dessalegn Rahmato. March 2003.

No. 2   *Faces of poverty: Life in Gäta, Wälo.* By Harald Aspen. June 2003

No. 3   *Destitution in Rural Ethiopia.* By Yared Amare. Forthcoming, 2003

www.ingramcontent.com/pod-product-compliance
Lightning Source LLC
Chambersburg PA
CBHW050615290326

41929CB00063B/2913